Collins | streetfinder

YO...

Contents

Key to street map symbols	2
Key to street map pages	3
City centre map	4-5
Street maps	6-27
Local information	28-29
Places of interest	30-33
The Minster	34
Key to road map symbols	35
Road map	36-37
Index to street names	38-48

Published by Collins
An imprint of HarperCollins*Publishers*
77-85 Fulham Palace Road, Hammersmith, London W6 8JB

www.collins.co.uk

Copyright © HarperCollins*Publishers* Ltd 2005

Collins® is a registered trademark of HarperCollins*Publishers* Limited

Mapping generated from Collins Bartholomew digital databases

The grid on the mapping pages is the National Grid taken from the Ordnance Survey map with the permission of the Controller of Her Majesty's Stationery Office.

Printed in China

ISBN 0 00 717002 5
Imp 001   QI11613 / CDDM

e-mail: roadcheck@harpercollins.co.uk

2 Key to street map symbols

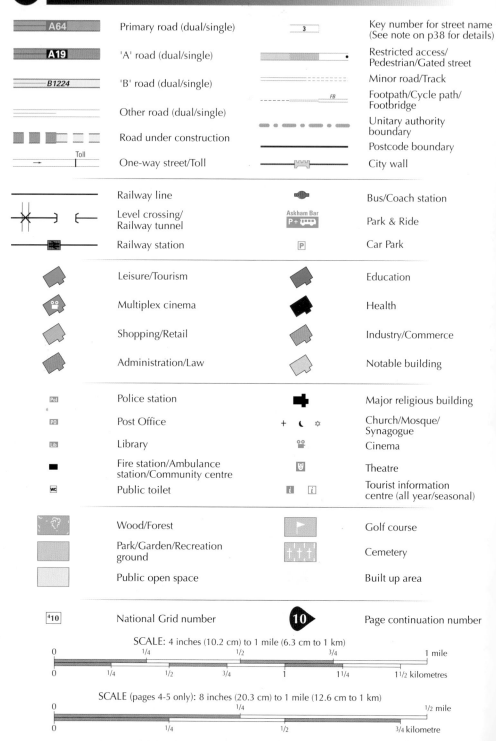

A64	Primary road (dual/single)	3	Key number for street name (See note on p38 for details)
A19	'A' road (dual/single)		Restricted access/ Pedestrian/Gated street
B1224	'B' road (dual/single)		Minor road/Track
	Other road (dual/single)	FB	Footpath/Cycle path/ Footbridge
	Road under construction		Unitary authority boundary
Toll	One-way street/Toll		Postcode boundary
			City wall

	Railway line		Bus/Coach station
	Level crossing/ Railway tunnel	Askham Bar P+	Park & Ride
	Railway station	P	Car Park

	Leisure/Tourism		Education
	Multiplex cinema		Health
	Shopping/Retail		Industry/Commerce
	Administration/Law		Notable building

Pol	Police station		Major religious building
PO	Post Office	+ ☾ ✡	Church/Mosque/ Synagogue
Lib	Library		Cinema
	Fire station/Ambulance station/Community centre		Theatre
WC	Public toilet	i i	Tourist information centre (all year/seasonal)

	Wood/Forest		Golf course
	Park/Garden/Recreation ground		Cemetery
	Public open space		Built up area

⁴10	National Grid number	10	Page continuation number

SCALE: 4 inches (10.2 cm) to 1 mile (6.3 cm to 1 km)

0   1/4   1/2   3/4   1 mile
0   1/4   1/2   3/4   1   1¼   1½ kilometres

SCALE (pages 4-5 only): 8 inches (20.3 cm) to 1 mile (12.6 cm to 1 km)

0   1/4   1/2 mile
0   1/4   1/2   3/4 kilometre

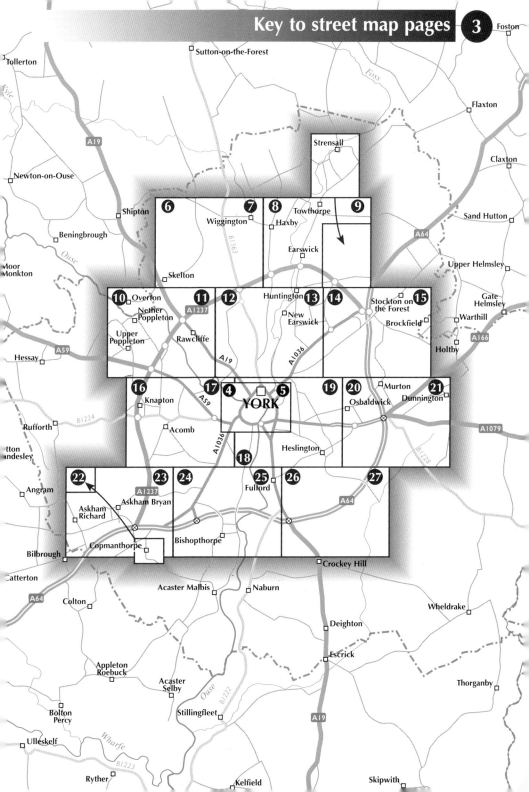

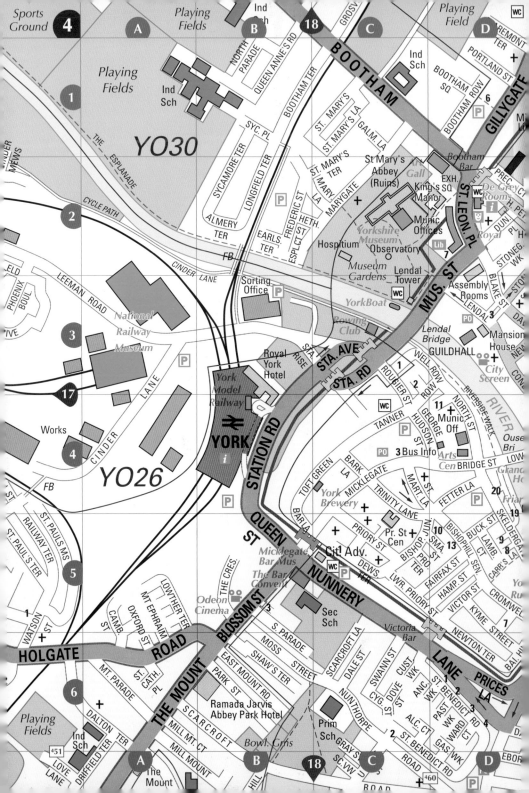

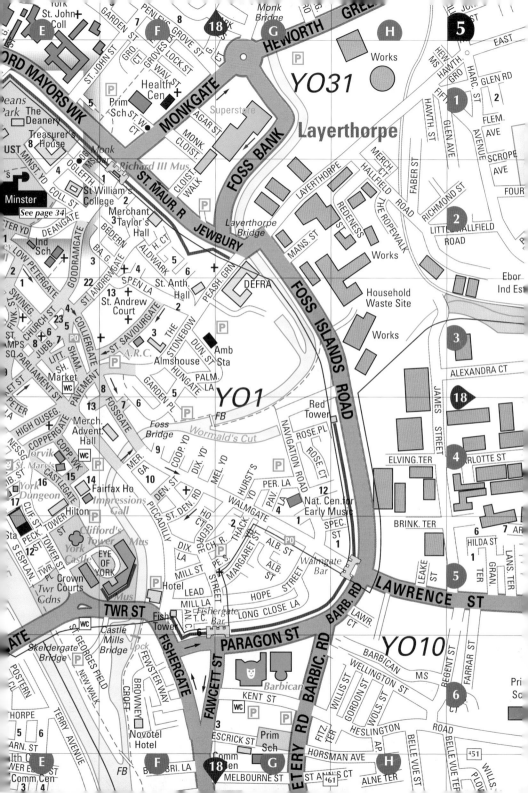

Rifle Ranges

TOWTHORPE

STRENSALL PARK

STRENSALL PARK

Playing Field

Tennis Courts

STRENSALL PARK

TOWTHORPE LANE

Ground

ANDRA ROAD

Army Medical Services Training Centre

Cemetery

SHERIFF HUTTON ROAD

Earswick Grange

Works

Works

CHURCH LA

Prim Sch

HAXBY MOOR RD

CREASER CL

WESTPIT CL

WOODLEIGH CL

CHALD. CL

SHELLY DR

WILK LANE

WEST END

WEST WILK WAY

FOSSL GARTH

WORLD DRIVE

LOWCROFT

RIVERSIDE

WOODM

LYNWOOD WALK

MIDDLECROFT

MIDDLECR

GRO

GLEBE

STATION SQ

HA CLO

MOOR LANE

YORK RD

PRINCESS ROAD

ORCHARD WAY

FB

DURLSTON DR

SIM. CL

SUSSEX CT

LANGTON RISE

PEL. WY

PEL PL

MELCOMBE AVE

TOBY CL

PORTISHAM PL

KIRKLANDS

HIGH AVE

ASH WK

HALL WY

OAKLANDS

THE WILLO

OAK TREE CLOSE

OAK TREE WAY

THE BIR

FLAXTON ROAD

OAKHILL CRES

BALFOUR WAY

BARLEY BCH. PL

CORN- CFT

RYE- CROFT

WAINCFT

YORK

KNAPTON CLOSE

NEWT. WAY

WILFRIDS RD

OX

HOWARD

CARR AVE

DR

HUMBER ROAD

CUMB

HOLLIS CRES

Football Ground

SCOTT MONCRIEFF ROAD

PASTURE CL

WHIN CL

LANE

CHESHIRE AVENUE

FARRIERS CHASE

ST BORDER RD

Comm Cen

Queen Elizabeth Barracks

Sports Ground

ALEXANDRA ROAD

STRENSALL PARK

STRENSALL

MONKS

NETHER WOODS

THE

SOUTHFIELDS ROAD

Lib

PO

VILLAGE

THE ROAD

NORTHFIELDS

BLACKLEE CL

CHARLES CT

Village Hall

JAYWICK LANE

TERR. CT

CHATS

CHAUCER GDN

RENE GRN

DARF DR

CLOSE

DUN AVE

LAKES CLOSE

WOB GDNS

GAINS

HEATH FO

WALTH CL

RIDE

MORAYN CL

GREEN LA

HAPMAN CL

PULLEYN CL

TUDOR WAY

FOLD WK

LITTLETH LANE

GATE

THE PA

BRECKS

LORDS MOOR LANE

Clubhouse

YO32

STRENSALL

YORK GOLF COURSE

Pol

Playing Field

1

2

3

4

5

6

7

8

9

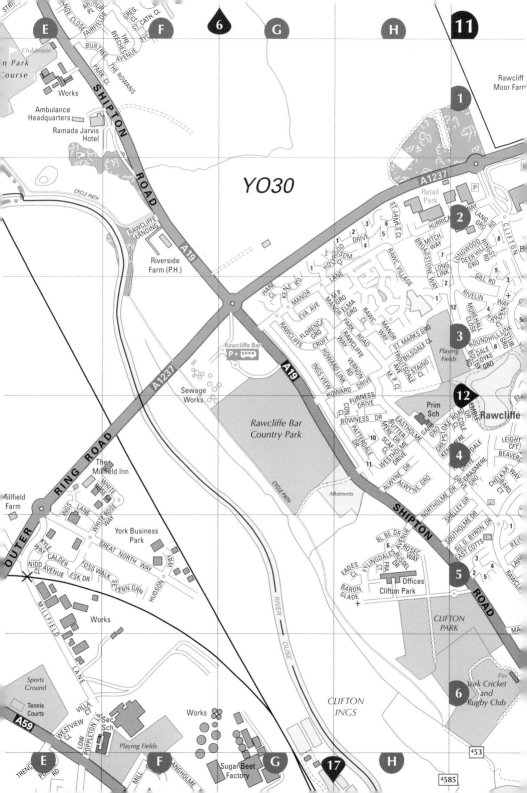

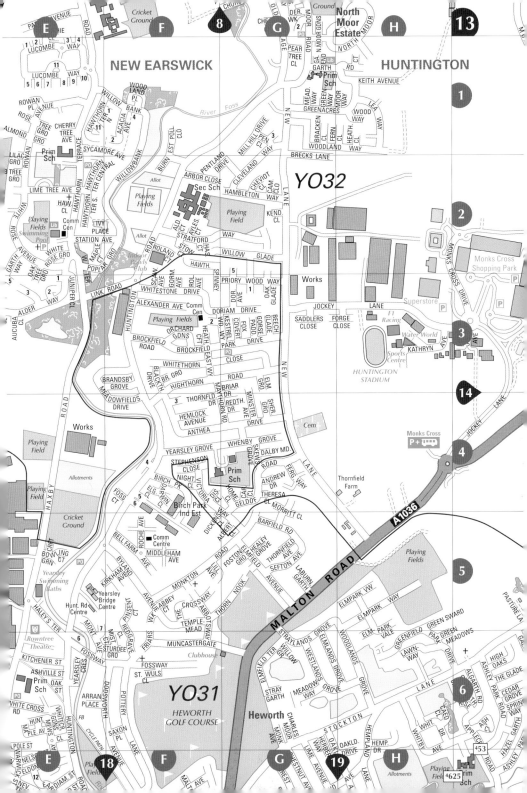

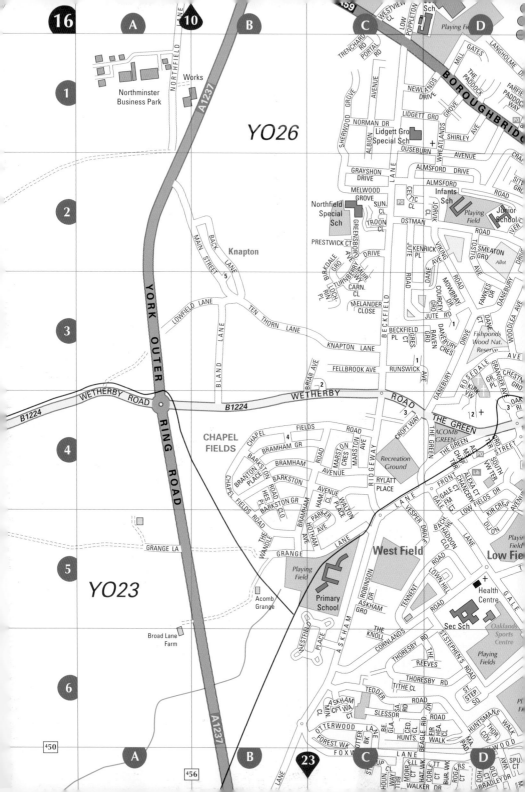

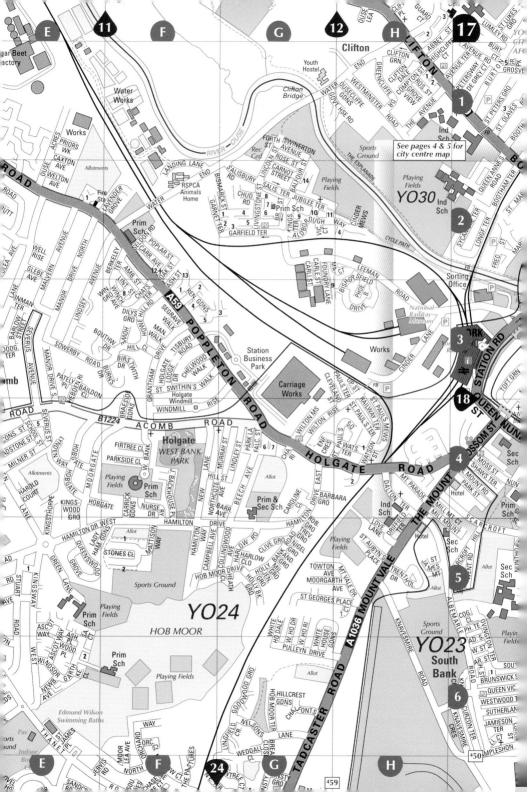

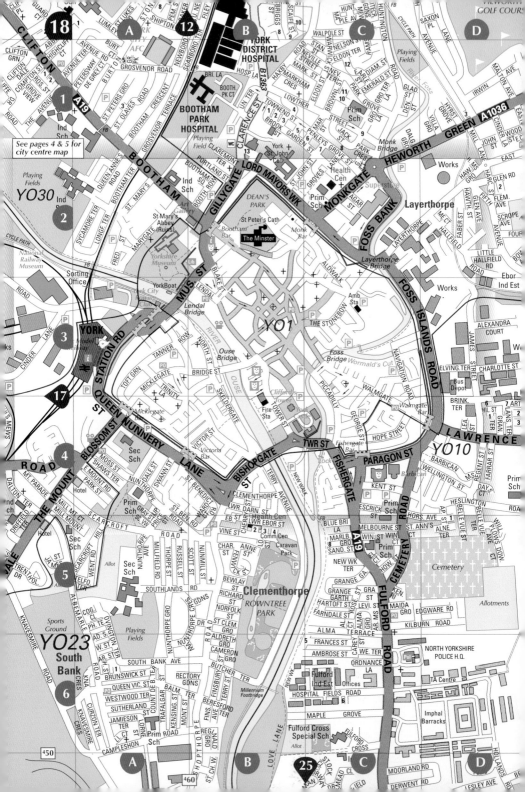

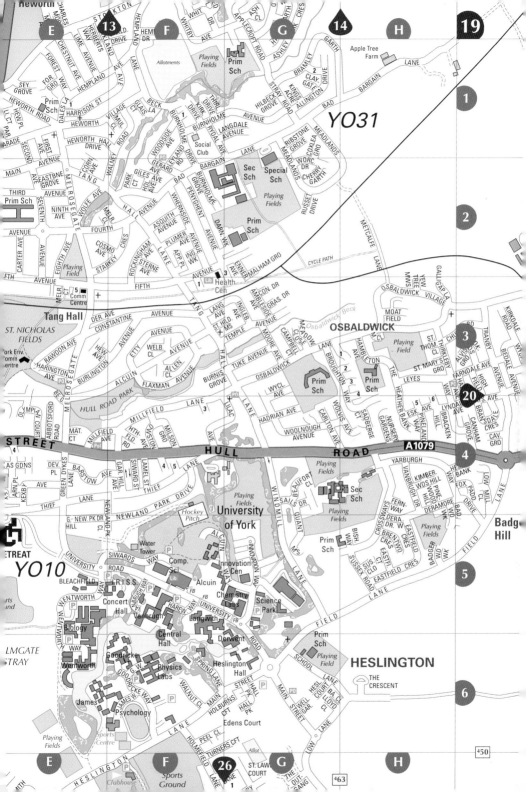

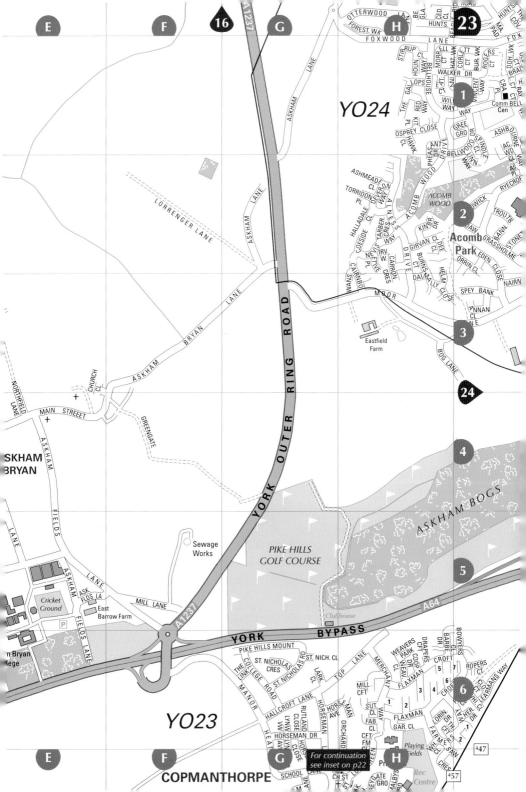

For continuation see inset on p22

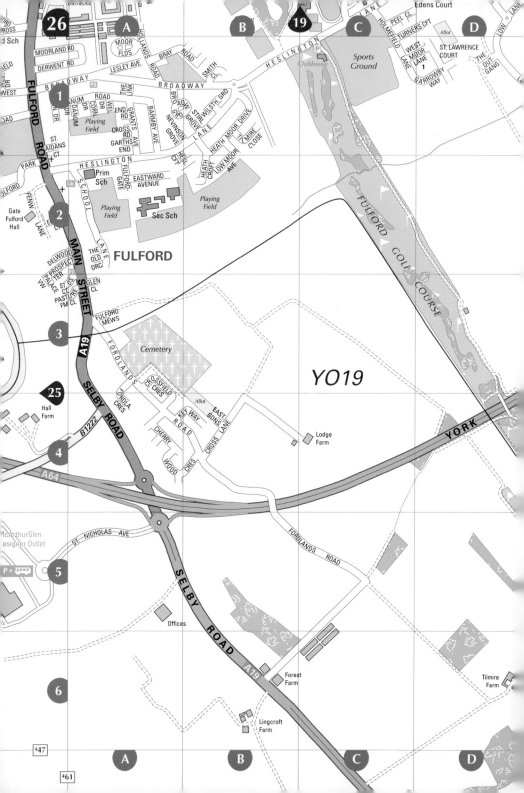

USEFUL INFORMATION

Crematorium
Bishopthorpe Road, Middlethorpe YO23 2QD
Tel: 01904 706096 **25 F4**

Central Library
Library Square, Museum Street YO1 7DS
Tel: 01904 552815 **4 D2**

Main Post Office
22 Lendal YO1 8DA *Tel: 01904 617285*
www.royalmail.com **4 D3**

North Yorkshire Police
Headquarters, Fulford Road YO10 4BY
Tel: 01904 631321
www.northyorkshire.police.uk **18 C6**

Tourist Information Centres
Tel: 01904 621756
www.york-tourism.co.uk

De Grey Rooms, Exhibition Square YO1 2HB **4 D2**

York Railway Station, Station Road YO1 7HB **4 B4**

ADMINISTRATION

City of York Council
The Guildhall YO1 9QN
Tel: 01904 613161 www.york.gov.uk **4 D3**

Commercial Services Department
Foss Islands Depot, Foss Islands Road YO31 7ZR **5 G3**

Community Services, Customer Advice Centre
10-12 George Hudson Street YO1 6ZE **4 C4**

Educational Services
Mill House, North Street YO1 7ZR **4 D4**

Environment and Development Services
9 St Leonard's Place YO1 7ET **4 D2**

Leisure Services
18 Back Swinegate, Swinegate Court YO1 8ZD **5 E3**

Resources Group
City Finance Centre, Library Square YO1 7DU **4 D2**

ENTERTAINMENT

Cinemas
City Screen, Coney Street YO1 9QL
Tel: 01904 541144/541155
www.picturehouses.co.uk **4 D3**

Odeon Cinema, Blossom Street YO24 1AJ
Tel: 01904 623287 www.odeon.co.uk **4 B5**

Vue, Clifton Moor Centre, Stirling Road, YO30 4XY
Tel: 08712 240240
www.myvue.com **12 A2**

Theatres
Barbican Centre, Paragon Street YO10 4NT
Tel: 01904 628991 Booking Office 01904 656688 **5 G6**

Friargate Theatre, Lower Friargate YO1 9SL
Tel: 0845 916 3000 www.ridinglights.org **5 E4**

Grand Opera House, 4 Cumberland Street YO1 9SW
Tel: 01904 655441 Booking Office 01904 671818 **5 E4**

Joseph Rowntree Theatre, Haxby Road YO31 8XY
Tel: 01904 658197 **13 E5**
www.jrtheatre.co.uk

Theatre Royal, St.Leonards Place YO1 7HD
Tel: 01904 623568/610041
www.theatre-royal-york.co.uk **4 D2**

FURTHER EDUCATION

Askham Bryan College, Askham Bryan YO23 3FR
Tel: 01904 772277
www.askham-bryan.ac.uk **23 E6**

The College of Law, Bishopthorpe Road Y023 2GA
Tel: 0800 318130/01904 682000
www.college-of-law.co.uk **25 F3**

York St John College (Uni of Leeds)
Lord Mayor's Walk YO31 7EX *Tel: 01904 624624*
www.yorksj.ac.uk **5 E1**

University of York, Heslington YO10 5DD
Tel: 01904 430000 www.york.ac.uk **19 F5**

York College, Tadcaster Road, Dringhouses YO24 1UA
Tel: 01904 770200
www.yorkcollege.ac.uk **24 D3**

HEALTH

York Health Services NHS Trust
Bootham Park Hospital, Bootham YO30 7BY
Tel: 01904 631313 **18 B1**

York District Hospital, Wiggington Road YO31 8HE
Tel: 01904 631313 A & E Department **12 D6**

Tees, East and N Yorkshire Ambulance Service NHS Trust
Ambulance Headquarters, Fairfields, Shipton Road
YO30 1XW *Tel: 01904 666000* **11 E1**

Independent Hospitals
Pury Cust Nuffield Hospital, Precentor's Court YO1 7EL
Tel: 01904 641571
www.nuffieldhospitals.org.uk **4 D2**

Stockton Hall Hospital, The Village, Stockton on the Forest
YO32 9UN *Tel: 01904 400500* **15 F1**

The Retreat, 107 Heslington Road YO10 5BN
Tel: 01904 412551
www.retreat-hospital.org **19 E5**

HELP AND ADVICE

Citizens Advice Bureau,
3 Blossom Street YO24 1AU
Tel: 01904 636066
www.yorkcab.org.uk **4 C5**

Samaritans, 89 Nunnery Lane YO23 1AH
Tel: 01904 655888 www.samaritans.org.uk **4 C5**

Victim Support, 15 Priory Street YO1 6ET
Tel: 01904 636905/0845 3030900
www.victimsupport.com **4 C5**

National Helplines

Missing Persons *Tel: 0500 700 700*
www.missingpersons.org

Childline *Tel: 0800 1111*
www.childline.org.uk

NSPCC Child Protection *Tel: 0808 800500*
www.nspcc.org.uk

Rape Crisis Federation *Tel: 0115 900 3560*
www.rapecrisis.co.uk

RSPCA *Tel: 0870 3335999* www.rspca.org.uk

MEDIA

Local Newspapers

York & County Press *Tel: 01904 653051*
www.yorkandcountypress.co.uk
York Advertiser (weekly)
York Star (weekly)
Yorkshire Evening Press (daily)
Yorkshire Gazette & Herald (weekly)
Yorkshire Post (daily) *Tel: 0113 243 2701*
www.yorkshiretoday.co.uk

Local Radio

Minster FM FM104.7 MHz
Tel: 01904 488888 www.minsterfm.com

BBC Radio York FM 95.5,103.7,104.3 MHz
& AM 666 & 1260 kMz
Tel: 01904 641351
www.bbc.co.uk/england/radioyork

SPORT & LEISURE

Association Football

York City F.C., Bootham Crescent YO30 7AQ
Tel: 01904 624447 www.ycfc.net **18 A1**

Golf

Fulford Golf Club, Heslington Lane, Heslington YO10 5DY
Tel: 01904 413579
www.fulfordgolfclub.co.uk **26 C1**

Forest of Galtres Golf Club, Skelton Lane, Wigginton
YO32 3RF *Tel: 01904 766198*
www.forestofgaltres.co.uk **6 C3**

Heworth Golf Club, Muncaster House, Muncastergate
YO31 9JY *Tel: 01904 422389* **13 G6**

Pike Hills Golf Club, Tadcaster Road YO23 3UW
Tel: 01904 700797 **23 G5**

Horse Racing

York Racecourse YO23 1EX *Tel: 01904 620911*
www.yorkracecourse.co.uk **25 F1**

Motor Racing

1 Racing Premier Karting, Monks Cross YO32 9JS
Tel: 01904 673555 www.karting.uk.com **13 H3**

Rugby League

York City Knights, Huntington Stadium, Kathryn Avenue
YO32 9JS *Tel: 01904 656105* **13 H3**

Sports & Leisure Centres/Swimming Pools

Barbican Centre, Barbican Road YO10 4NT
Tel: 01904 630266 **5 G6**

Edmund Wilson Swimming Pool, Thanet Road, Acomb
YO24 2NW *Tel: 01904 793031* **17 E6**

Huntington Stadium, Kathryn Avenue, Huntington YO32 9JS
Tel: 01904 642111 **13 H3**

Oaklands Sports Centre, Cornlands Road, Acomb
YO24 3DX *Tel: 01904 782841* **16 D5**

Water World, Kathryn Avenue, Monk's Cross YO32 9XX
Tel: 01904 642111 **13 H3**
www.waterworldyork.co.uk

Yearsley Swimming Pool, Haley's Terrace, Haxby Road
YO31 8SB *Tel: 01904 622773* **13 E5**

Shopping

Shopmobility, Piccadilly Car Park, Coppergate Centre
Tel: 01904 679222
www.disabilityuk.com **5 E4**

Clifton Moor, Stirling Road YO30 4XZ
Tel: 01904 690206 **12 A2**

Coppergate Centre, Coppergate YO1 9NT
Tel: 01904 627160 **4 E4**

McArthurglen Designer Outlet, St Nicholas Ave, Fulford
YO19 4TA *Tel: 01904 682720*
www.mcarthurglen.com **25 H5**

Monks Cross Shopping Park, Monks Cross Drive,
Huntington YO32 9GX *Tel: 01904 623374*
www.monkscross.net **14 A2**

Newgate Market YO1 7LA *(open daily)*
Tel: 01904 551355 **5 E3**

Bookshops

Blackwells, University of York, Heslington YO10 5DU
Tel: 01904 432715 www.blackwells.co.uk **19 F5**

Borders Books and Music, 1/5 Davygate YO1 8QY
Tel: 01904 653300
www.bordersstores.co.uk **4 D3**

Waterstone's www.waterstones.co.uk
28/29 High Ousegate YO1 8RX *Tel: 01904 628740* **5 E4**
9/10 High Ousegate YO1 8RZ *Tel: 01904 653300* **5 E4**

W.H.Smith www.whsmith.co.uk
39/41 Coney Street YO1 9QL *Tel: 01904 623106* **4 D3**
Monks Cross Shopping Park YO32 9GX
Tel: 01904 622555 **14 A2**
York District Hospital, Wigginton Road YO31 8HE
Tel: 01904 620368 **14 A2**

TRANSPORT

Bus Services

BusInfo Centre, 20 George Hudson Street YO1 6WR
Tel: 01904 551400 **4 C4**

Dial and Ride *Tel: 01904 624455*
York Wheels *Tel: 01904 630080*

Coach Parks

Union Terrace, Clarence Street YO31 **18 B1**
Kent Street YO10 *Tel: 01904 632735* **5 G6**

Lorry Park

Burton Lane **20 D2**

Park & Ride

Askham Bar *Tel: 01904 883100* **24 C3**
Grimston Bar *Tel: 01904 883090* **20 B4**
McArthurglen Designer Outlet (Mon to Sat)
Tel: 01904 435637 **25 H5**
Monks Cross *Tel: 01904 640854* **13 H4**
Rawcliffe Bar *Tel: 01904 883990* **11 G3**

Rail

Railway Station, Station Road YO24 1AB **4 B4**
National Rail Enquiries *Tel: 08457 484950*
www.nationalrail.co.uk

Indicates a place of interest that appears in the street map pages. An explanation of the other symbols can be found on page 35.

Abbey House Museum   36 A5
The museum, housed partly in the gatehouse of the 12c church at Kirkstall, includes reconstructed Victorian streets with houses, shops and workshops furnished with period artefacts and exhibitions about the social history of Leeds and Kirkstall Abbey. *Tel: 0113 230 5492*
www.leeds.gov.uk/abbeyhouse

Allerton Park   36 C3
A 19c mansion in a large park with lakes, to the north east of Knaresborough.

ARC   5 F3
A hands-on archaeology resource centre in the medieval church of St. Saviour in York city centre. There are opportunities to sort and date authentic finds, plan an excavation using computers, and try the ancient crafts of spinning and weaving.
Tel: 01904 543403
www.jorvik-viking-centre.co.uk

Barley Hall   5 E2
The medieval oak-framed home of Alderman Snawsell restored to how it would have been in the 1480's using authentic materials and techniques. Located off Stonegate in the heart of York.
Tel: 01904 610275

Battle of Boroughbridge 1322   36 C2
A battle site, where the rebellious Earl of Lancaster was defeated and executed by his cousin, Edward II, after hostilities broke out.

Battle of Marston Moor 1644   36 C3
The scene of the largest battle of this Civil War. The Royalists, led by Prince Rupert, were defeated by the Parliamentarians and lost control of the North.

Battle of Myton 1319   36 C2
The battle site where Edward II was defeated by the Scots during Scottish Wars of Independence. Rare documentation from the time shows military tactics used in this period.

Battle of Stamford Bridge 1066   37 F3
The battle site, where Harold II defeated and killed his brother, Tostig, and Norwegian claimant to English throne, Harald Hardrada.

Battle of Towton 1461   36 C5
A battle site, where reputedly the largest and bloodiest battle ever fought on English soil took place. The Yorkists, led by Edward, Earl of March, defeated the Lancastrians, leaving 28,000 dead.

Beningbrough Hall   36 D3
The house was built by John Bourchier in 1716 (National Trust), with fine plasterwork and wood carving. It is set in a large park with gardens to the north west of Beningbrough. The Georgian Hall is hung with over 100 pictures from the National Portrait Gallery.
Tel: 01904 470666
www.nationaltrust.org.uk

Bramham Park   36 C4
A 18c classical mansion surrounded by grounds modelled on those of Versailles, to the south west of Bramham.
Tel: 01937 846000

Brimham Rocks   36 A2
A large group of rocks (National Trust) which have been fantastically shaped by erosion, to the east of Pateley Bridge.
Tel: 01423 780688

Burnby Hall   37 G4
The two lakes display 80 varieties of hardy water lilies, which have been designated a National Collection. There is also a sporting trophy museum.
Tel: 01759 302068
www.burnbyhallgardens.co.uk

Byland Abbey   36 D1
The ruins of a 12c Cistercian monastery (English Heritage) located at the hamlet of Byland Abbey. The ruin of the church has a striking west front and notable patterned floor tiles.
Tel: 01347 868614
www.english-heritage.org.uk

Castle Howard   37 F1
A baroque 18c mansion by Vanbrugh surrounded by large formal grounds. It contains fine collections of furniture, paintings, ceramics and statuary.
Tel: 01653 648444
www.castlehoward.co.uk

Clifford's Tower   5 E5
The remains of a 13c-14c stone tower (English Heritage) in a quatrefoil design, forming part of the York Castle fortifications. Built by Henry III to replace William the Conqueror's wooden keep which was razed in 1190, it sits atop a layered Norman motte, dominating York's skyline and affording fine views of the city.
Tel: 01904 646940
www.cliffordstower.com

Eden Camp   37 F1
A former prisoner of war camp, located to the north east of Malton, which recreates life in Britain during World War II by means of light, sound, smell and smoke.
Tel: 01653 697777
www.edencamp.co.uk

Fairfax House   5 E4
A museum of 18c life with a fine collection of period furniture and clocks in a Georgian town house in Castlegate.
Tel: 01904 655543
www.fairfaxhouse.co.uk

Fountains Abbey   36 A2
The remains of this medieval Cistercian abbey (National Trust and English Heritage) beside the River Skell, are part of a World Heritage Site. The nearby, Fountains Hall, is a 17c house largely built with materials from the ruins of the abbey.
Tel: 01765 608888
www.fountainsabbey.org.uk

Gilling Castle 37 E1
The original 14c house has both Tudor and Georgian alterations, which is now a preparatory school for Ampleforth College. There are fine gardens in the grounds.

Golden Acre Park 36 A4
The 137 acres of gardens, lake and woodland to the south east of Bramhope were originally a large amusement park in the 1930s. The site is now a garden of botanical interest with rock, cottage and demonstration gardens. There is also a Display House for tender plants, old shrub roses, a pinetum and an arboretum. The park is notable for its spring and autumn colour.

Harewood House 36 B4
A mansion built in the 18c and 19c with landscaped grounds laid out by 'Capability' Brown. The formal Italian-style terrace was designed by Charles Barry in 1840.
Tel: 0113 218 1010
www.harewood.org

Harlow Carr (RHS) 36 A3
Set in 68 acres which are landscaped with woodland, herbaceous, rock, bog and alpine gardens. There is also a Museum of Gardening and a model village.
Tel: 01423 565418
www.rhs.org.uk

Headingley 36 A5
Home to Yorkshire County Cricket Club and a Test match venue.
Tel: 0113 278 7394
www.yorkshireccc.org.uk

Impressions Gallery 5 E4
Located in a Georgian townhouse the gallery has contemporary photographic and new media exhibitions.
Tel: 01904 654724
www.impressions-gallery.com

Isurium Roman Town 36 C2
A small Roman town with a rectangular layout, on the north side of Aldborough. Some fragments of the town wall remain, and there are some interesting mosaics.

Jorvik 5 E4
Time capsules fly visitors inches above a dynamic reconstruction of Jorvik, the 10c Viking City of York. A combination of modern technology and real archeological evidence brings the trading hub of the Viking world to life.
Tel: 01904 643211 (24 hrs)
www.jorvik-viking-centre.co.uk

Jorvik Glass 37 F2
Demonstrations of glass-blowing and gift shop located in the grounds of Castle Howard.
Tel: 01653 648555
www.jorvikglass.co.uk

Kirkham Priory 37 F2
Augustinian priory dating from the 12c (English Heritage), in the Derwent valley, south west of Malton. The late 13c gatehouse has magnificent heraldic shields.
Tel: 01653 618768
www.english-heritage.org.uk

Kirkstall Abbey 36 A5
The remains of 12c Cistercian church (English Heritage) by the River Aire, north west of Leeds. The gatehouse is now a museum. *www.kirkstall.org.uk/abbey*

Knaresborough Castle 36 B3
The ruined 14c castle of John of Gaunt, partly demolished by Roundheads. On the cliff top close to the market place in Knaresborough.
www.knaresborough.co.uk/castle

Lightwater Valley Park 36 A1
Located to the north west of Ripon. The attraction has rollercoaster rides, parkland, a farm and factory shopping outlets.
Tel: 0870 458 0040
www.lightwatervalley.co.uk

Lotherton Hall 36 C5
The former home of Lord and Lady Gascoigne, was completed at the beginning of the 20c. There is a museum of decorative arts containing the Gascoigne family's collection of paintings, jewellery, porcelain and silver. In the grounds there are formal Edwardian gardens. Wildlife on the estate includes two deer herds and a collection of over 200 bird species.
Tel: 0113 281 3259

Markenfield Hall 36 A2
A turreted moated farmhouse dating from 14c. The original seat of the Markenfield family, which was forfeited by Sir Thomas Markenfield following his involvement in the 1569 rebellion against Queen Elizabeth I.
Tel: 01845 597 226
www.markenfield.com

Merchant Adventurers' Hall 5 F4
The 14c Guildhall with a notable timbered Great Hall, in Fossgate.
Tel: 01904 654818
www.theyorkcompany.co.uk

Micklegate Bar Museum 4 C5
This 800-year-old royal gateway to York, in the city walls, houses a museum that portrays a civil and social insight into the history of York through scenic, graphic and tableaux format.
Tel: 01904 634436   www.micklegatebar.co.uk

Mother Shipton's Cave 36 B3
Located in Knaresborough Gorge, a legendary prophetess was reputed to have lived here in 15c, who predicted the invention of motor cars and aeroplanes. There is also a Petrifying Well, museum, playground and 12 acres of riverside grounds.
Tel: 01423 864600   www.mothershipton.co.uk

☐ **National Railway Museum**   4 A2
The railway heritage museum in York, is the largest in the world. There is a historic collection of locomotives and rolling stock including Mallard, the world's fastest steam locomotive, and Queen Victoria's personal saloon.
Tel: 01904 621261
www.nrm.org.uk

✠ **Newburgh Priory**   36 D1
There are remains of a monastery in the grounds of this 18c mansion.

▦ **Newby Hall**   36 B2
An 18c house, with interiors partly by Adam, which have recently been restored. The estate borders River Ure, to the west of Boroughbridge. The grounds contain the National Collection of Cornus plants.
Tel: 01423 322583
www.newbyhall.co.uk

▨ **Norton Conyers**   36 B1
Dating from medieval times with Stuart and Georgian additions, the house was visited by Charlotte Brontë and is linked to the novel, 'Jane Eyre'. The 18c walled garden has an orangery.
Tel: 01765 640333

▦ **Nunnington Hall**   37 E1
This 17c manor and walled garden (National Trust) on the south side of the River Rye in the Vale of Pickering contains the Carlisle Collection of Miniature Rooms.
Tel: 01439 748283
www.nationaltrust.org.uk

✠ **Old Malton Church**   37 F1
A 12c parish church, with a notable west front, north east of Malton. There are also relics of a Gilbertine priory founded circa 1150.
Tel: 01653 600048

▥ **Ripley Castle**   36 A2
Located in Ripley Park, the castle was re-built in 1780, however the 15c gatehouse and 16c tower remain. The grounds were designed by 'Capability' Brown with the gardens containing the National Collection of Hyacinths, along with spring bulbs and tropical plants.
Tel: 01423 770152
www.ripleycastle.co.uk

✠ **Ripon Cathedral**   36 B1
This 12c cathedral, with a Saxon crypt, is noted for the choir stalls and range of building styles from Saxon to Perpendicular.
Tel: 01765 603462
www.riponcathedral.org.uk

⚐ **Ripon Racecourse**   36 B2
Flat-racing course, with thirteen race days a year, which encircles a lake on the west side of the River Ure, to the south east of Ripon.
Tel: 01765 602156
www.ripon-races.co.uk

★ **Roman Ridge**   36 C5
Roman road running from the Great North Road, east of Upton, through Castleford and Tadcaster, to York.

▥ **Royal Armouries Museum**   36 B5
Displays the history of armour and arms from 5BC to modern times, located in the centre of Leeds with five themed galleries; Orient, Hunting, Self-Defence, Tournament and War. There are demonstrations of jousting, falconery and poleaxe combat. Leatherworkers and gunmakers can be found in the Craft Centre and there is also a Menagerie.
Tel: 0113 220 1916   www.armouries.org.uk

✠ **Selby Abbey**   37 E5
An 11c limestone abbey with three towers.
Tel: 01757 703123
www.selbyabbeyappeal.btinternet.co.uk

▨ **Shandy Hall**   36 D1
A mid-15c house and garden on the west side of Coxwold. The house was the home of the 18c parson Lawrence Sterne, author of 'Tristram Shandy', between 1760 and 1768 and it contains the world's foremost collection of Sterne's novels. There is also a walled garden with old roses and a wild garden in an old quarry.
Tel: 01347 868465

▥ **Spofforth Castle**   36 B3
The remains of a 14c fortified manor house owned by Percy family (English Heritage) west of Spofforth.
Tel: 0191 2611585   www.english-heritage.org.uk

▦ **Steeton Hall**   36 C5
Remains of a medieval castle, situated west of South Milford. The gatehouse (English Heritage), probably dates from the 14c, and is well-preserved.
Tel: 01904 601901   www.english-heritage.org.uk

▦ **Stockeld Park**   36 B4
A small mansion designed by James Paine in Palladian style for the Middleton family, in the 18c and set in a large estate.
Tel: 01937 586101   www.harrogate.gov.uk

▨ **Studley Royal**   36 A2
The 18c water garden contains ornamental lakes, temples and statues. The estate includes the remains of the manor house which burnt down in 1945. St. Mary's Church (English Heritage), with it's highly decorated interior was designed in the 1870s by William Burges, but is no longer used for worship.
Tel: 01765 608888
www.fountainsabbey.org.uk

▨ **Sutton Park**   36 D2
Early Georgian house, on the south side of Sutton-on-the-Forest. The house has magnificent plasterwork by Cortese and an important collection of porcelain and 18c furniture. The parkland was designed in a similar style to 'Capability' Brown, there are award winning gardens with a lily canal and woodland walks.
Tel: 01347 810249
www.statelyhome.co.uk

Temple Newsam   36 B5
A Tudor and Jacobean house and museum set in 1200 acres of parkland. The house contains a large collection of Chippendale furniture, a notable Picture Gallery and an 18c State Bed. The grounds include formal gardens, mixed woodland and Home Farm which is a rare breeds centre. *Tel: 0113 264 7321*
www.leeds.gov.uk/templenewsam

The Bar Convent   4 B5
Home of England's oldest active convent community, with museum illustrating York's early Christian history and life of the convent. Situated in Blossom Street, it contains a magnificent 18c domed chapel with priest's hiding hole. *Tel: 01904 643238*
www.bar-convent.org.uk

The Minster (see p34)   5 E2
The largest medieval Gothic cathedral in Europe. The building was started in 1220, and took two-and-a-half centuries to complete. Noted for its stained glass, particularly the large east window, and rose window in south transept. The roof of the south transept was destroyed by fire in 1984; it was rebuilt using traditional methods. *Tel: 01904 557216*
www.yorkminster.org

Thicket Priory   37 E4
A Carmelite nunnery on the site of a 12c monastery, located to the south east of Wheldrake. *Tel: 01904 448277*
www.carmelite.org.uk

Treasurer's House   5 E1
Dating mainly from the 17c and 18c, although medieval in origin and once home of the Treasurers of York Minster. A fine collection of period furniture, china and glass. *Tel: 01904 624247*
www.nationaltrust.org.uk

Tropical World   36 B5
In Roundhay Park, north east of Leeds city centre, this attraction includes tropical plant houses which contain tropical fauna and flora, a butterfly house, a nocturnal house, and Coronation House with changing plant displays. *Tel: 0113 266 1850*

Wetherby Racecourse   36 C4
Located to the north east of Wetherby, adjacent to the A1 trunk road. National Hunt course, with fourteen race days a year. *Tel: 01937 582035*
www.wetherbyracing.co.uk

Wharram Percy Village   37 G2
A deserted former medieval village (English Heritage) with only the church ruin remaining. *Tel: 01904 601901*
www.english-heritage.org.uk

Wyville Animal Farm   37 F1
A working family farm with rare and older breeds, from cows to guinea pigs. Attractions include a farm shop, museum and local crafts. *Tel: 01653 928930*

York Castle Museum   5 F5
Located in York's old prison buildings in Tower Street, recording everyday life through the centuries and including a cobbled Victorian street full of shops, costume, social history, and military collections. *Tel: 01904 687687*
www.yorkcastlemuseum.org.uk

York City Art Gallery   4 D2
Paintings from the 15c to 20c including works by Bellotto, Reynolds, Lowry, Nash and York-born William Etty. Housed in a 19c Renaissance style building in Exhibition Square, York. There is also a collection of 20c studio pottery. *Tel: 01904 697979*
www.yorkartgallery.org.uk

York Dungeon   5 E4
Museum of horrors in Clifford Street. Exhibits include the evocation of The Plague and encounters with Dick Turpin and Guy Fawkes. *Tel: 01904 632599*
www.thedungeons.com

York Racecourse   25 E2
Flat-racing course with fifteen race days each year, including the Ebor meeting in August and will host Royal Ascot in 2005. *Tel: 01904 620911*
www.yorkracecourse.co.uk

York St. Mary's   5 E4
The 14c church in Castlegate now houses changing exhibitions for York Museum Trust. *Tel: 01904 687687*

Yorkshire Air Museum   37 E4
Over 30 historic aircraft, including a Halifax bomber, and aircraft equipment and memorabilia displayed at World War II bomber base, north east of Elvington. Airborne Forces Museum, Barnes Wallis Collection and a restored control tower with sound effects. *Tel: 01904 608595*
www.yorkshireairmuseum.co.uk

Yorkshire Museum   4 C2
Collections of Roman, Viking, Anglo-Saxon and medieval artefacts including the 15c Middleham Jewel, a gold pendant set with large sapphire; also decorative arts and natural history exhibits. *Tel: 01904 687687*
www.yorkshiremuseum.org.uk

Yorkshire Museum of Farming   20 C2
An assortment of tools and machinery along with rare breeds of farm animals. There is also a reconstruction of James Herriot's surgery, blacksmith's shop, chapel, hardware shop and Land Army display. Other features include the Derwent Valley Light Railway, a Brigantium reconstruction of a Roman fort, a Danelaw reconstruction of a Dark Ages village, a gift shop, cafe and picnic/play area. *Tel: 01904 489966*

The triple towers of the great Minster dominate York. The fifth church to stand upon the site, it is built on cruciform style and its chief characteristics, inside as outside, are great beauty and impressive size and space. The magnificent stained glass in the Minster - much of it medieval - is of tremendous interest. In the south transept the great Rose window displays a design entwining the red and white roses of Lancaster and York respectively, commemorating the wedding in 1486 of Henry VII to Elizabeth of York, which at last united the two warring 'Roses.' The Choir, the north transept and the octagonal Chapter House are very fine, the roof vaulting being among the best examples to be seen anywhere. Beyond the Close to the north of the Minster are the Deanery and the Library (Early English), the latter the depository of many literary treasures. The Minster itself is rich in historic possessions and is the seat of the second See of England, its Archbishop being next in rank and precedence to the Primate of All England, Archbishop of Canterbury. A fire in 1984 badly damaged the roof of the south transept but brave firefighting prevented it from spreading to the rest of the Cathedral.

DEANS PARK

The Library & Archives

The Deanery

City Walls

Gray's Court

Minster Court

❶ Altar of The Lord's Prayer
❷ Nave Pulpit
❸ Nave Altar
❹ St. John's Chapel
❺ Five Sisters Window
❻ St. Nicholas' Chapel
❼ Astronomical Clock
❽ Vestibule
❾ Effigy of Prince William of Hatfield
❿ St. Stephen's Chapel
⓫ Tomb of Archbishop Scrope
⓬ All Saint's Chapel
⓭ Entrance to Crypt
⓮ High Altar
⓯ Zouche Chapel
⓰ Archbishop Thomson Monument
⓱ Tomb of Archbishop Walter de Grey
⓲ Dean Duncombe Monument
⓳ St. George's Chapel
⓴ Bookshop

Treasurer's House

CHAPTER HOUSE STREET

OGLEFORTH

CHAPTER HOUSE

Site of former Chapel of St. Mary and the Holy Angels

NORTH TRANSEPT

N.W. Nave Door

NORTH AISLE

NORTH CHOIR AISLE

CHOIR

LADY CHAPEL

EAST END

St. William's College

COLLEGE ST

Great West Door

WEST END

NAVE

S.W. Nave Door

SOUTH AISLE

SOUTH CHOIR AISLE

Vestry & Registry

SOUTH TRANSEPT

South Door

Vestry

Treasury

THE QUEEN'S PATH

St. Michael-le-Belfry

MINSTER YARD

HIGH PETERGATE

MINSTER GATES

Roman Column

DEANGATE

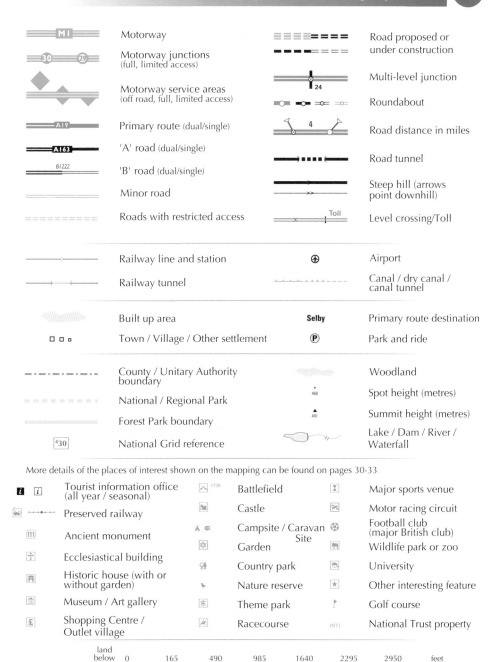

Motorway

Motorway junctions
(full, limited access)

Motorway service areas
(off road, full, limited access)

Primary route (dual/single)

'A' road (dual/single)

'B' road (dual/single)

Minor road

Roads with restricted access

Railway line and station

Railway tunnel

Built up area

Town / Village / Other settlement

County / Unitary Authority
boundary

National / Regional Park

Forest Park boundary

National Grid reference

Road proposed or
under construction

Multi-level junction

Roundabout

Road distance in miles

Road tunnel

Steep hill (arrows
point downhill)

Level crossing/Toll

Airport

Canal / dry canal /
canal tunnel

Primary route destination

Park and ride

Woodland

Spot height (metres)

Summit height (metres)

Lake / Dam / River /
Waterfall

More details of the places of interest shown on the mapping can be found on pages 30-33

Tourist information office
(all year / seasonal)

Preserved railway

Ancient monument

Ecclesiastical building

Historic house (with or
without garden)

Museum / Art gallery

Shopping Centre /
Outlet village

Battlefield

Castle

Campsite / Caravan
Site

Garden

Country park

Nature reserve

Theme park

Racecourse

Major sports venue

Motor racing circuit

Football club
(major British club)

Wildlife park or zoo

University

Other interesting feature

Golf course

National Trust property

| | land below | 0 | 165 | 490 | 985 | 1640 | 2295 | 2950 | feet |
| water | sea level | 0 | 50 | 150 | 300 | 500 | 700 | 900 | metres |

SCALE: 4 miles to 1 inch (2.54cm) / 10km to 4cm approx

| 0 | | 4 | | 8 | | 12 | | 16 miles |
| 0 | 5 | | 10 | | 15 | | 20 | | 25 kilometres |

General Abbreviations

All	Alley	Conv	Convent	Gdn	Garden	Ms	Mews	Sec	Secondary
Allot	Allotments	Cor	Corner	Gdns	Gardens	Mt	Mount	Shop	Shopping
Amb	Ambulance	Coron	Coroners	Govt	Government	Mus	Museum	Sq	Square
App	Approach	Cors	Corners	Gra	Grange	N	North	St.	Saint
Arc	Arcade	Cotts	Cottages	Grd	Ground	NT	National	St	Street
Ave	Avenue	Cov	Covered	Grds	Grounds		Trust	Sta	Station
Bdy	Broadway	Crem	Crematorium	Grn	Green	Nat	National	Sts	Streets
Bk	Bank	Cres	Crescent	Grns	Greens		Trust	Sub	Subway
Bldgs	Buildings	Ct	Court	Gro	Grove	PH	Public House	Swim	Swimming
Boul	Boulevard	Cts	Courts	Gros	Groves	PO	Post Office	TA	Territorial
Bowl	Bowling	Ctyd	Courtyard	Gt	Great	Par	Parade		Army
Br/Bri	Bridge	Dep	Depot	Ho	House	Pas	Passage	TH	Town Hall
C of E	Church of	Dev	Development	Hos	Houses	Pav	Pavilion	Tenn	Tennis
	England	Dr	Drive	Hosp	Hospital	Pk	Park	Ter	Terrace
Cath	Cathedral	Dws	Dwellings	Hts	Heights	Pl	Place	Thea	Theatre
Cem	Cemetery	E	East	Ind	Industrial	Pol	Police	Trd	Trading
Cen	Central,	Ed	Education	Int	International	Prec	Precinct	Twr	Tower
	Centre	Elec	Electricity	Junct	Junction	Prim	Primary	Twrs	Towers
Cft	Croft	Embk	Embankment	La	Lane	Prom	Promenade	Uni	University
Cfts	Crofts	Est	Estate	Las	Lanes	Pt	Point	Up	Upper
Ch	Church	Ex	Exchange	Lib	Library	Quad	Quadrant	Vil	Villa, Villas
Chyd	Churchyard	Exhib	Exhibition	Lo	Lodge	RC	Roman	Vw	View
Cin	Cinema	FB	Footbridge	Lwr	Lower		Catholic	W	West
Circ	Circus	FC	Football Club	Mag	Magistrates	Rd	Road	Wd	Wood
Cl	Close	Fld	Field	Mans	Mansions	Rds	Roads	Wds	Woods
Co	County	Flds	Fields	Mem	Memorial	Rec	Recreation	Wf	Wharf
Coll	College	Fm	Farm	Mid	Middle	Res	Reservoir	Wk	Walk
Comm	Community	Gall	Gallery	Mkt	Market	Ri	Rise	Wks	Works
Comn	Common	Gar	Garage	Mkts	Markets	S	South	Yd	Yard
						Sch	School		

District Abbreviations

A.Bry.	Askham Bryan	Hes.	Heslington	St.For.	Stockton on the Forest
A.Rich.	Askham Richard	Hunt.	Huntington	Stren.	Strensall
Bish.	Bishopthorpe	Midd.	Middlethorpe	Tow.	Towthorpe
Cop.	Copmanthorpe	N.Ears.	New Earswick	U.Pop.	Upper Poppleton
Drin.	Dringhouses	N.Pop.	Nether Poppleton	Wig.	Wigginton
Dun.	Dunnington	Osb.	Osbaldwick		
Ears.	Earswick	Skel.	Skelton		

There are entries in the index which are followed by a number in **bold**. These numbers can be found on the map where there is insufficient space to show the street name in full. For example the location of Abbot St **6** *YO31* 18 C1, will be found by a number **6** in the square C1 on page 18.

A

Abbey Ct *YO31*	13	F5	Aldreth Gro *YO23*	18	B6	Annan Cl *YO24*	24	A3
Abbey St *YO30*	17	H1	Aldwark *YO1*	5	F2	Anne St *YO23*	18	B5
Abbotsford Rd *YO10*	19	E4	Alexa Ct *YO24*	16	D4	Anson Dr *YO10*	25	H1
Abbots Gait (Hunt.) *YO32*	8	C5	Alexander Av *YO31*	13	F3	Anthea Dr *YO31*	13	F4
Abbot St **6** *YO31*	18	C1	Alexandra Ct *YO10*	18	D3	Apollo Ct **1** *YO10*	18	D5
Abbotsway *YO31*	13	F5	Alexandra Rd (Stren.) *YO32*	9	F6	Apollo St *YO10*	5	H6
Abelton Gro (Haxby) *YO32*	8	A3	Algarth Ri *YO31*	14	A6	Appleby Glade (Haxby) *YO32*	8	A4
Acacia Gro (Haxby) *YO32*	8	A2	Algarth Rd *YO31*	14	A6	Appleby Pl *YO31*	19	F2
Acaster La (Bish.) *YO23*	25	F5	Allanson Gro **2** *YO24*	17	F5	Applecroft Rd *YO31*	14	A6
Acomb Ms (Acomb) *YO24*	16	D4	Allan St **2** *YO30*	12	D6	Apple Garth (U.Pop.) *YO26*	10	C4
Acomb Rd *YO24*	17	F4	Allen Cl *YO10*	19	F3	Appleton Ct (Bish.) *YO23*	24	D6
Acomb Wd Cl *YO24*	24	A1	Allendale *YO24*	24	B1	Appleton Rd (Bish.) *YO23*	24	D6
Acomb Wd Dr *YO24*	23	H2	Allerton Dr (N.Pop.) *YO26*	10	C3	Arbor Cl (Hunt.) *YO32*	13	F2
Acorn Way *YO24*	24	B1	Allington Dr *YO31*	19	G1	Arenhall Cl **1** (Wig.) *YO32*	7	H3
Adelaide St *YO23*	18	A6	Alma Ct *YO10*	18	C5	Argyle St *YO23*	18	A6
Adlington Cl **3** (Stren.) *YO32*	9	F4	Alma Gro *YO10*	18	C5	Arlington Rd *YO30*	12	B4
Agar St *YO31*	5	F1	Alma Ter *YO10*	18	C5	Arncliffe Ms *YO10*	18	C5
Ainsty Av *YO24*	24	D1	Almery Ter *YO30*	4	B2	Arnside Pl *YO10*	19	E4
Ainsty Gro *YO24*	24	D1	Almond Gro (N.Ears.) *YO32*	13	E1	Arran Pl *YO31*	13	E6
Aintree Ct *YO24*	24	D1	Almsford Dr *YO26*	16	C2	Arthur Pl (Skel.) *YO30*	6	A6
Albany St **7** *YO26*	17	G2	Almsford Rd *YO26*	16	D2	Arthur St *YO10*	18	D4
Albemarle Rd *YO23*	17	H5	Alness Dr *YO24*	23	H2	Arundel Gro *YO24*	24	A2
Albert Cl (Hunt.) *YO32*	13	F5	Alne Ter *YO10*	18	D5	Ascot Rd (Wig.) *YO32*	7	G1
Albert St *YO10*	5	G5	Alvis Gro *YO10*	20	A3	Ascot Way *YO24*	17	E6
Albion Av *YO26*	16	C2	Alwyne Dr *YO30*	11	H4	Ashbourne Pl *YO24*	24	A2
Albion St **9** *YO1*	4	D5	Alwyne Gro *YO30*	11	H4	Ashbourne Way *YO24*	24	A1
Alcelina Ct *YO23*	4	C6	Amberly St *YO26*	17	F2	Ash Cl *YO31*	14	A6
Alcuin Av *YO10*	19	F3	Amber St **12** *YO31*	18	C1	Ashdale Rd (Dun.) *YO19*	21	H2
Alcuin Way (Hes.) *YO10*	19	F5	Ambleside Av *YO10*	19	G3	Ashfield Ct **2** *YO24*	24	C2
Aldborough Way *YO26*	17	G2	Ambrose St *YO10*	18	C6	Ashford Pl *YO24*	17	E5
Alderley Ct (Hunt.) *YO32*	13	F2	Amy Johnson Way *YO30*	12	A2	Ashley Pk Cres *YO31*	19	G1
Aldersyde *YO24*	24	C2	Ancress Wk *YO23*	4	C6	Ashley Pk Rd *YO31*	14	A6
Aldersyde Ct *YO24*	24	C2	Ancroft Cl *YO1*	5	F5	Ashmeade Ct *YO24*	23	H2
Aldersyde Ms **3** *YO24*	24	C2	Anderson Gro *YO24*	17	G5	Ash St *YO26*	17	F3
Alder Way (N.Ears.) *YO32*	13	E3	Andrew Dr (Hunt.) *YO32*	13	G4	Ashton Av *YO30*	12	C5
			Angram Cl *YO30*	12	A4	Ashville St *YO31*	13	E6

Ash Wk (Stren.) YO32	9	G5
Ashwood Glade (Haxby) YO32	7	H5
Askham Bryan La (A.Bry.) YO23	23	F3
Askham Cft YO24	16	C6
Askham Flds La (A.Bry.) YO23	23	E4
Askham Gro YO24	16	C5
Askham La YO24	23	G1
Aspen Cl (Dun.) YO19	21	H1
Asquith Av YO31	19	F2
Atcherley Cl YO10	25	G1
Atlas Rd YO30	12	B2
Aucuba Cl (N.Ears.) YO32	13	E3
Audax Cl YO30	12	B2
Audax Rd YO30	12	B2
Auster Rd YO30	12	B2
Avenue, The YO30	17	H1
Avenue, The (Haxby) YO32	7	H1
Avenue, The (Park Est) YO32	8	A3
Avenue Rd YO30	18	A1
Avenue Ter YO30	17	H1
Aviator Ct YO30	12	A3
Avon Dr (Hunt.) YO32	8	C5
Aylesham Ct (Hunt.) YO32	13	F2

B

Bachelor Hill YO24	16	D5
Backhouse St 1 YO31	18	B1
Back La (Cop.) YO23	22	A2
Back La (Knapton) YO26	16	B2
Back La (Wig.) YO32	7	G2
Back Swinegate 2 YO1	5	E3
Back W Vw 8 YO30	12	C6
Bad Bargain La YO31	19	F2
Badger Paddock 2 YO31	13	F3
Badger Wd Wk YO10	19	H5
Baildon Cl YO30	17	E3
Baile Hill Ter YO1	4	D6
Baker St YO30	12	C6
Balfour St YO26	17	G2
Balfour Way (Stren.) YO32	9	F5
Balmoral Ter YO23	18	A6
Bankside Cl (U.Pop.) YO26	10	C3
Bannisdale YO24	24	A2
Barbara Gro YO24	17	G4
Barbers Dr (Cop.) YO23	22	B1
Barbican Ms YO10	5	H6
Barbican Pl YO10	5	G6
Barbican Rd YO10	5	G5
Barden Cl YO30	12	A4
Barfield Rd YO31	13	G5
Barker La YO1	4	C4
Barkston Av YO26	16	B4
Barkston Cl YO26	16	B4
Barkston Gro YO26	16	B5
Barkston Rd YO26	16	B4
Bar La YO1	4	B4
Barleycorn Yd 10 YO1	5	F4
Barley Ri (Stren.) YO32	9	F5
Barley Vw (Haxby) YO32	7	H3
Barley Vw (Wig.) YO32	7	H3
Barlow St YO26	17	E3
Barmby Av YO10	26	A1
Barmby Cl 7 YO30	12	A4
Barnfield Way (Cop.) YO23	22	A3
Baron Glade YO30	11	H5
Barons Cres (Cop.) YO23	22	B2
Barrett Av YO24	17	F4
Barstow Av YO10	19	E4
Bartle Garth YO1	5	F2
Bateson Cl (Hes.) YO10	19	G6
Baysdale Av YO10	20	A4
Beaconsfield Ms 6 YO24	17	E4
Beaconsfield St YO24	17	E4
Beadle Garth (Cop.) YO23	22	B2
Beagle Ridge Dr YO24	16	C6
Beans Way YO31	14	A5
Beaufort Cl YO10	19	G4
Beaulieu Cl (Hunt.) YO32	8	C6
Beaverdyke YO30	12	A4
Beckfield La YO26	16	C3
Beckfield Pl YO26	16	C3
Beck La YO31	19	F1
Beckside Gdns YO10	19	E4
Beckwith Cl 1 YO31	14	B6
Bedale Av YO10	20	A3
Bede Av YO30	12	C6

Bedern YO1	5	F2
Beech Av (Bish.) YO23	25	E6
Beech Av YO24	17	G4
Beeches, The (Skel.) YO30	6	B6
Beech Glade YO31	13	G3
Beech Gro (Acomb) YO26	16	D3
Beech Gro (U.Pop.) YO26	10	B4
Beech Pl (Stren.) YO32	9	F5
Beech Way (U.Pop.) YO26	10	C4
Beechwood Glade YO24	16	C6
Beeforth Cl 3 (N.Ears.) YO32	13	E1
Belcombe Way 10 YO32	12	B6
Belgrave St YO31	12	D6
Bell Cl (Wig.) YO32	7	H3
Belle Vue St YO10	5	H6
Belle Vue Ter YO10	18	D4
Bell Fm Av YO31	13	F5
Bellhouse Way YO24	23	H1
Bellmans Cft (Cop.) YO23	22	B2
Bellwood Dr YO24	23	H1
Belmont Cl YO30	12	A4
Bentley Pk (Osb.) YO10	20	A3
Beresford Ter YO23	18	B6
Berkeley Ter YO26	17	F2
Beverley Ct 2 YO24	17	E6
Beverley Gdns 3 YO31	18	D1
Bewlay St YO23	18	B5
Bilsdale Cl YO30	11	H3
Birch Cl 1 (N.Ears.) YO32	13	E3
Birch Copse 1 YO32	17	E5
Birches, The (Stren.) YO32	9	G4
Birch La (Haxby) YO32	8	A2
Birch Pk YO31	13	F4
Birch Tree Cl 4 (Stren.) YO32	9	F5
Birch Tree Ct 3 (Haxby) YO32	8	A2
Birkdale Gro YO26	16	C3
Birstwith Dr YO26	17	F3
Bishopfields Dr YO26	17	H3
Bishopgate St YO23	4	D6
Bishophill Jun YO1	4	C5
Bishophill Sen YO1	4	D5
Bishops Way YO10	19	H5
Bishopthorpe Rd YO23	25	G1
Bismarck St YO10	17	F2
Black Dikes La (U.Pop.) YO26	10	B5
Black Horse Pas 6 YO1	5	F4
Blacklee Cl (Stren.) YO32	9	H2
Blackthorn Dr YO31	13	F3
Blakeley Gro 8 YO30	12	A2
Blakeney Pl YO10	18	D4
Blake St YO1	4	D2
Bland La YO26	16	B3
Blatchford Ct 14 YO30	12	C5
Blatchford Ms 13 YO30	12	C5
Bleachfield (Hes.) YO10	19	E5
Blenheim Ct 2 YO30	11	G2
Bleriot Way YO30	12	B2
Blossom St YO24	4	B6
Blue Beck Dr YO30	11	H5
Blue Br La YO10	18	C5
Board St 3 YO23	18	B5
Bog La YO24	23	H3
Bollans Ct 3 YO1	5	F2
Boltby Rd YO30	12	A3
Bonnington Ct 2 YO26	17	F3
Bootham YO30	4	C1
Bootham Bar YO1	4	D2
Bootham Cres YO30	18	A1
Bootham Pk Ct YO31	18	B1
Bootham Row YO30	4	D1
Bootham Sq YO30	4	D1
Bootham Ter YO30	4	B1
Boothwood Rd 12 YO30	12	A3
Border Rd (Stren.) YO32	9	F6
Boroughbridge Rd YO26	11	E6
Borrowdale Dr YO30	12	A4
Bouthwaite Dr YO26	17	F3
Bowes Av YO31	18	D2
Bowland Way YO30	12	B4
Bowling Grn Ct YO31	13	E5
Bowling Grn Cft YO31	13	E5
Bowling Grn La 9 YO31	18	C1
Bowness Dr YO30	11	H4
Bowyers Cl (Cop.) YO23	22	C1
Bracken Cl (Hunt.) YO32	13	G1
Bracken Hill YO30	19	H4
Brackenhills (U.Pop.) YO26	10	C4
Bracken Rd YO24	24	D2
Bradley Dr YO24	24	A1

Braeside Gdns YO24	17	F4
Brailsford Cres YO30	12	B5
Bramble Dene YO24	24	B2
Bramble Gro (Hunt.) YO31	13	F3
Bramham Av YO26	16	B4
Bramham Gro YO26	16	B5
Bramham Rd YO26	16	B5
Bramley Garth YO31	19	G1
Brandon Gro YO32	14	D2
Brandsby Gro YO31	13	F3
Bransdale Cres YO10	20	A4
Bransholme Dr YO30	12	B3
Branton Pl YO26	16	B4
Bray Rd YO10	26	A1
Breary Cl YO24	17	G6
Brecks Cl 4 (Wig.) YO32	7	H3
Brecksfield (Skel.) YO30	6	B6
Brecks La (Hunt.) YO32	13	G1
Brentwood Cres YO10	19	H5
Bretgate 1 YO1	5	G5
Briar Av YO26	16	C3
Briar Dr YO31	13	G4
Bridge Cl (Haxby) YO32	7	H4
Bridge La YO31	18	B1
Bridge Rd (Bish.) YO23	24	D6
Bridge St YO1	4	D4
Bridle Way 4 YO26	16	B4
Briergate (Haxby) YO32	8	A4
Briggs St YO31	12	D6
Bright St YO26	17	G2
Brinkworth Ter YO10	5	H5
Broad Acres (Haxby) YO32	7	H4
Broad Oak La 7 (Wig.) YO32	7	G2
Broadstone Way YO30	11	H2
Broadway YO10	25	H1
Broadway Gro YO10	26	A1
Broadway W YO10	25	H1
Brockfield Pk Dr YO31	13	F3
Brockfield Rd YO31	13	F3
Bromley St 8 YO26	17	G2
Brompton Rd YO30	12	B6
Brooklands YO10	20	A3
Brook St YO31	18	B1
Broome Cl (Hunt.) YO32	8	C6
Broome Rd 1 (Hunt.) YO32	8	D6
Broome Way (Hunt.) YO32	8	D6
Brougham Cl 3 YO30	12	A5
Broughton Way YO10	19	G3
Browney Cft YO10	5	F6
Brownlow St YO31	18	C1
Brunel St 9 YO26	17	G2
Brunswick St YO23	18	A6
Buckingham Ct 10 YO1	4	D5
Buckingham St YO1	4	D5
Buckingham Ter 13 YO1	4	D5
Bull La YO10	19	E4
Bull La (Heworth) YO31	19	E1
Burdyke Av YO30	12	B5
Burgess Wk YO24	24	A1
Burlands La (U.Pop.) YO26	10	B6
Burlington Av YO10	19	E3
Burn Est (Hunt.) YO32	13	F2
Burnholme Av YO31	19	F1
Burnholme Dr YO31	19	F1
Burnholme Gro YO31	19	F2
Burniston Gro YO10	19	F3
Burnsall Dr YO26	17	F3
Burns Ct YO24	23	H2
Burrill Av YO30	12	C5
Burrill Dr (Wig.) YO32	7	F2
Burton Av YO30	12	C6
Burton Ct YO30	18	A1
Burton Grn YO30	12	C5
Burton Stone La YO30	18	A1
Burtree Av (Skel.) YO30	18	E1
Butcher Ter YO23	18	B6
Buttacre La (A.Rich.) YO23	22	B5
Butter Cl 4 (Wig.) YO32	7	G2
Buttermere Dr YO30	11	H4
Butt Hill 6 (Wig.) YO32	7	G2
Byland Av YO31	13	F5
Byron Dr YO30	12	A5

C

Caedmon Cl YO31	13	H6
Cairnborrow YO24	23	H2
Caithness Cl 1 YO30	11	H2

Name	Page	Grid
Caldbeck Cl YO30	12	B4
Calder Av (N.Pop.) YO26	11	E5
Calf Cl (Haxby) YO32	8	B3
Calvert Cl (Hunt.) YO32	7	H4
Cambrian Cl (Hunt.) YO32	13	G2
Cambridge St YO24	4	A5
Cameron Gro YO23	18	B6
Campbell Av YO24	17	F5
Campbell Cl YO10	19	G3
Campleshon Rd YO23	18	A6
Canham Gro YO10	20	A4
Canterbury Cl 9 (Wig.) YO32	7	G1
Carey St YO10	18	C6
Carleton St YO26	17	G2
Carlisle St YO26	17	G2
Carl St 4 YO23	18	B5
Carlton Av YO10	19	G4
Carlton Cotts 11 (Wig.) YO32	7	G1
Carmelite St 5 YO1	5	F3
Carmires Av (Haxby) YO32	8	B2
Carnot St YO26	17	G2
Caroline Cl YO10	17	G4
Caroline St 1 YO23	18	B5
Carrfield YO24	24	A1
Carrick Gdns YO24	17	F4
Carrington Av YO26	17	F2
Carr La YO26	17	E3
Carrnock Cl (Hunt.) YO32	13	G4
Carron Cres YO24	23	H2
Carrs La YO1	4	D5
Carter Av YO31	19	E2
Castle Cl (Wig.) YO32	7	F1
Castlegate YO1	5	E4
Castle Mills Br YO1	5	F5
Castle Wk 14 YO1	5	E4
Catherine Ct 6 YO10	18	D4
Cavendish Gro YO10	20	A4
Caxton Av YO26	17	E1
Cayley Cl YO30	12	A4
Cecilia Pl 1 YO24	17	H4
Cedar Glade (Dun.) YO19	21	G2
Cedar Gro YO31	14	A6
Cedarwood Cl YO24	16	C6
Celtic Cl YO26	16	C2
Cemetery Rd YO10	18	C5
Centurion Pk YO30	12	C3
Chaldon Cl (Stren.) YO32	9	F5
Chalfonts YO24	17	G6
Chaloners Cres YO24	24	B2
Chaloners Rd YO24	24	B1
Chancery Ct (Acomb) YO24	16	D4
Chancery Ri YO24	17	G4
Chantry Av (U.Pop.) YO26	10	C4
Chantry Cl YO24	24	A2
Chantry Gap (U.Pop.) YO26	10	C4
Chantry Gro (U.Pop.) YO26	10	C4
Chantry La (Bish.) YO23	25	F5
Chapel Flds Rd YO26	16	B4
Chapel La (A.Bry.) YO23	22	D4
Chapel Row YO1	5	G5
Chapel Ter YO24	16	D4
Chapman's Ct YO24	24	B3
Chapter Ho St 4 YO1	5	E2
Charles Ct (Stren.) YO32	9	H3
Charles Moor YO31	13	G6
Charlotte St YO10	18	D3
Charlton St YO23	18	B5
Chaseside Ct YO24	24	C1
Chatsworth Av (Stren.) YO32	9	H2
Chatsworth Dr (Haxby) YO32	8	C2
Chatsworth Ter YO26	17	F3
Chaucer La (Stren.) YO32	9	H2
Chaucer St 3 YO10	18	D4
Chaumont Way (St.For.) YO32	15	F1
Chelkar Way YO30	12	A4
Chelwood Wk YO26	17	F3
Cherry Garth YO31	19	G2
Cherry Gro 3 (U.Pop.) YO26	10	C4
Cherry Hill La 11 YO23	4	E6
Cherry La YO24	24	D1
Cherry Orchard 8 (Haxby) YO32	8	A3
Cherry Paddock (Haxby) YO32	8	A3
Cherry St YO23	18	B5
Cherry Tree Av (N.Ears.) YO32	13	E1
Cherry Tree Ct 3 (Dun.) YO19	21	G2
Cherry Wd Cres (Fulford) YO19	26	A4
Cheshire Av (Stren.) YO32	9	F6
Chesney Flds YO24	17	E6
Chessingham Gdns YO24	24	C3
Chestnut Av YO31	19	E1
Chestnut Ct (Hunt.) YO32	8	C6
Chestnut Gro (Acomb) YO26	16	D3
Chestnut Gro 4 (N.Ears.) YO32	13	F1
Chestnuts, The 2 (Wig.) YO32	7	H3
Cheviot Cl (Hunt.) YO32	13	G2
Chiltern Way (Hunt.) YO32	8	C6
Chipstead Wk 7 (Stren.) YO32	9	F4
Chudleigh Rd YO26	17	G2
Church Balk (Dun.) YO19	21	G1
Church Cl (A.Bry.) YO23	23	E3
Churchfield Dr (Wig.) YO32	7	H2
Church La YO1	4	D4
Church La (Dun.) YO19	21	G1
Church La (Bish.) YO23	25	E5
Church La (N.Pop.) YO26	10	D3
Church La (Skel.) YO30	6	A6
Church La (Hunt.) YO32	8	C6
Church La (Stren.) YO32	9	F3
Church La (Wig.) YO32	7	H2
Church Ms 2 (Acomb) YO26	16	D4
Church Rd YO10	19	H3
Church St YO1	5	E3
Church St (Dun.) YO19	21	G1
Church St (Cop.) YO23	22	A2
Church Vw (Skel.) YO30	6	A5
Cinder La YO26	4	A4
Cinder La YO31	18	D1
Cinder Ms YO26	17	H2
Clarence St YO31	18	B1
Clarendon Ct YO31	12	D6
Clarendon St 5 YO31	12	D6
Clarks Ter 1 (Heworth) YO31	19	E1
Claygate YO31	19	G1
Clay Pl YO24	16	D6
Clementhorpe YO23	4	D6
Clement St 4 YO23	4	D6
Cleveland St YO24	17	G3
Cleveland Ter 3 (Hunt.) YO32	13	G1
Cleveland Way (Hunt.) YO32	13	G2
Clifford St YO1	5	E4
Clifton YO30	12	B6
Clifton Br YO26	17	G1
Clifton Br YO30	17	G1
Clifton Dale YO30	17	H1
Clifton Grn YO30	17	H1
Clifton Moor Gate YO30	12	A2
Clifton Moor Retail Pk YO30	12	B1
Clifton Pl YO30	12	B6
Clive Gro YO24	17	G5
Cloisters Wk YO31	5	F2
Cloither Ct (Cop.) YO23	22	C1
Close, The YO30	12	A5
Coda Av (Bish.) YO23	25	F6
Coeside YO24	23	H2
Coffee Yd YO1	5	E3
Coggan Cl YO23	18	A5
Coggan Way (Bish.) YO23	24	D5
Coledale Cl YO30	12	A4
Colenso St 5 YO23	5	E6
Cole St 3 YO31	18	B1
College Rd (Cop.) YO23	22	A1
College St YO1	5	E2
Colliergate YO1	5	E3
Collingham Pl 2 YO26	16	C3
Collingwood Av YO24	17	G5
Common La (Dun.) YO19	21	H6
Common Rd (Dun.) YO19	21	H1
Compton St YO30	17	H1
Concorde Way YO30	12	B2
Coneycroft (Dun.) YO19	21	H1
Coney St YO1	4	D3
Conifer Cl 5 (N.Ears.) YO32	13	E3
Coniston Cl YO30	11	H4
Coniston Dr YO10	19	G3
Connaught Ct YO10	25	H1
Connaught Way (Hunt.) YO32	8	C5
Constantine Av YO10	19	E3
Conway Cl 2 YO30	11	H2
Coopers Dr (Cop.) YO23	22	B1
Coopers Yd YO1	5	F4
Copmanthorpe La (Bish.) YO23	24	D6
Copper Beech Cl (Dun.) YO19	21	G1
Copper Beech Cl (U.Pop.) YO26	10	B5
Copper Beeches, The (Dun.) YO19	21	G1
Coppergate YO1	5	E4
Coppergate Wk YO1	5	E4
Coppice, The (Bish.) YO23	24	D5
Coppice Cl (Haxby) YO32	8	A1
Copwood Gro 5 (Wig.) YO32	7	H3
Corban La (Wig.) YO32	6	D1
Corban Way 5 (Wig.) YO32	7	G2
Corlett Ct YO24	24	A1
Cornborough Av YO31	19	E2
Corncroft (Stren.) YO32	9	F5
Corner Cl (Wig.) YO32	7	F2
Cornlands Rd YO24	16	C6
Cornwall Dr YO10	26	A1
Cornwood Way (Haxby) YO32	7	H3
Cosmo Av YO31	19	E2
Cotswold Way (Hunt.) YO32	8	D6
Cottage Ms 1 YO31	19	F1
Count de Burgh Ter YO23	18	A6
Courcey Gro YO26	16	D3
Courtyard, The (Bish.) YO23	25	E5
Covert, The YO24	24	D2
Coxlea Gro YO31	19	G1
Crab Tree Gro (N.Ears.) YO32	13	E2
Cranbrook Av YO26	16	D2
Cranbrook Rd YO26	16	D1
Cranefield Pl YO24	24	A1
Crawley Way 2 YO31	19	G1
Creaser Cl (Stren.) YO32	9	F4
Crescent, The (Hes.) YO10	19	H6
Crescent, The YO24	4	B5
Crescent Rd YO19	26	B4
Crichton Av YO30	12	C5
Crinan Ct (Hunt.) YO32	8	C5
Croft, The 1 (Stren.) YO32	9	G5
Croft Ct (Bish.) YO23	25	E5
Croft Fm Cl (Cop.) YO23	22	B1
Croft Side 3 YO23	16	C4
Croft Way YO26	16	C4
Crombie Av YO30	12	C6
Cromer St YO30	12	C6
Crompton Ter (Haxby) YO32	8	A5
Cromwell Rd YO1	4	D6
Crooklands La (Haxby) YO32	8	A1
Crossfield Cres (Fulford) YO19	26	A3
Crosslands Rd YO10	26	A1
Cross La (Fulford) YO19	26	B4
Cross La 4 YO24	16	D4
Crossway, The YO31	13	F5
Crossways YO10	19	H5
Crummock YO24	24	A2
Cumberland Cl 4 (Stren.) YO32	9	G5
Cumberland St YO1	5	E4
Cumbrian Av (Stren.) YO32	9	G5
Curlew Glebe (Dun.) YO19	21	G2
Curzon Ter YO23	18	A6
Custance Wk YO23	4	C6
Cycle St 4 YO10	19	F4
Cygnet St YO23	4	C6
Cyprus Gro (Haxby) YO32	7	H1
D		
Dalby Mead YO31	13	G4
Dale Dyke Gro YO30	12	A3
Dales La YO31	19	E1
Dale St YO23	4	C6
Dalguise Gro YO31	18	C1
Dalmally Cl YO24	23	H3
Dalton Ter YO24	4	A6
Damson Cl 5 YO26	17	F3
Dane Av YO24	16	D3
Danebury Ct YO26	16	D3
Danebury Cres YO26	16	D3
Danebury Dr YO26	16	D4
Danes Cft YO10	25	H1
Danesfort Av YO24	16	D5
Danesgate 1 YO26	16	D3
Danesmead Cl YO10	25	H1
Danum Dr YO10	26	A1
Danum Rd YO10	25	H1
Darbie Cl 5 (N.Ears.) YO32	13	E1
Darfield Cl (Stren.) YO32	9	H2
Darnborough St YO23	4	D6
Darnbrook Wk YO24	19	F2
Darwin Cl YO31	13	F4
Davygate YO1	4	D3

Name		
Daysfoot Ct *YO10*	18	D4
Deacons Ct (Cop.) *YO23*	22	B2
Dealtry Av (Wig.) *YO32*	7	H3
Deangate *YO1*	5	E2
Deanhead Gro **1** *YO30*	11	H3
Deans Cl (Bish.) *YO23*	24	D5
Deans Pk *YO1*	5	E1
Deepdale *YO24*	24	B1
Deer Hill Gro *YO30*	12	A2
Deerstone Way (Dun.) *YO19*	21	H2
De Grey Ct *YO31*	18	A1
De Grey Pl (Bish.) *YO23*	25	F6
De Grey St *YO31*	5	E1
De Grey Ter **13** *YO31*	18	B1
Delamere Cl (Wig.) *YO32*	7	G1
Dell, The (Skel.) *YO30*	6	A6
Del Pyke **5** *YO31*	18	B1
Delwood (Fulford) *YO10*	25	H2
De Mauley Pl (St.For.) *YO32*	15	F1
De Mowbray Ct (A.Rich.) *YO23*	22	A4
Dennison St *YO31*	18	C1
Dennis St *YO1*	5	F4
Deramore Dr *YO10*	19	H4
Deramore Dr W *YO10*	19	H5
Derwent Av *YO10*	19	E3
Derwent Bungalows **1** (Dun.) *YO19*	21	F2
Derwent Ct **2** (Dun.) *YO19*	21	F2
Derwent Est (Dun.) *YO19*	21	F2
Derwent La (Dun.) *YO19*	21	G2
Derwent Rd *YO10*	25	H1
Derwent Valley Estates (Dun.) *YO19*	21	H3
Derwent Wk (Hunt.) *YO32*	8	C6
Deveron Way *YO24*	23	H2
Devon Pl *YO10*	19	E4
Dewsbury Cotts **1** *YO1*	4	C5
Dewsbury Ter *YO1*	4	C5
Diamond St *YO1*	18	C1
Dickens Cl (Hunt.) *YO32*	13	F5
Dijon Av *YO24*	16	D5
Dikelands Cl (U.Pop.) *YO26*	10	C4
Dikelands La (U.Pop.) *YO26*	10	C3
Dike Ray Cl (Haxby) *YO32*	7	H4
Dilys Gro *YO26*	17	F3
Disraeli Ct (Hunt.) *YO32*	13	F4
Dixon La *YO1*	5	F5
Dixons Yd *YO1*	5	F4
Dodgson Ter *YO26*	17	E3
Dodsworth Av *YO31*	13	F6
Doe Pk *YO30*	12	A3
Doherty Wk *YO24*	24	A1
Don Av *YO24*	24	C1
Doriam Av *YO31*	13	G3
Doriam Dr *YO31*	13	F3
Dove St *YO23*	4	C6
Dower Ct *YO10*	18	D5
Drakes Cl (Hunt.) *YO32*	8	C6
Drake St **2** *YO23*	4	D6
Drapers Cft (Cop.) *YO23*	22	B1
Driffield Ter *YO24*	17	H5
Dringfield Cl *YO24*	24	B1
Dringthorpe Rd *YO24*	24	D2
Drome Rd (Cop.) *YO23*	22	C2
Drummond Vw (Bish.) *YO23*	25	F5
Dudley Ms **11** *YO31*	18	C1
Dudley St **10** *YO31*	18	C1
Duncombe Dr (Stren.) *YO32*	9	H2
Duncombe Pl *YO1*	4	D2
Dundas St *YO1*	5	F3
Durlston Dr (Stren.) *YO32*	9	F5
Dykes La (Cop.) *YO23*	22	A3

E

Name		
Eades Cl *YO30*	11	H5
Earle St *YO31*	18	C1
Earlsborough Ter *YO30*	4	B2
Earswick Chase (Ears.) *YO32*	8	C4
Earswick Village (Ears.) *YO32*	8	C4
Eason Rd *YO24*	24	C1
Eason Vw *YO24*	24	B1
Eastbourne Gro *YO31*	19	E2
East Cotts *YO30*	12	A5

Name		
Eastern Ct *YO31*	18	D1
Eastern Ter *YO31*	18	D1
Eastfield Av (Haxby) *YO32*	7	H4
Eastfield Cl *YO10*	19	H5
Eastfield Cres *YO10*	19	H5
Eastfield La (Dun.) *YO19*	21	G1
Eastholme Dr *YO30*	11	H4
Easthorpe Dr (N.Pop.) *YO26*	10	D4
Eastland Av **1** *YO24*	17	F5
Eastmoor Gdns (Fulford) *YO19*	26	B4
East Mt Rd *YO24*	4	B6
East Par *YO31*	18	D2
Eastward Av *YO10*	26	A2
East Way *YO31*	13	F3
Eaton Ct *YO24*	23	H1
Ebor Cl (U.Pop.) *YO26*	10	C4
Ebor St *YO23*	18	B5
Ebor Way (N.Pop.) *YO26*	10	C3
Ebor Way (U.Pop.) *YO26*	10	C3
Ebsay Dr *YO30*	12	A3
Eden Cl *YO24*	24	A2
Edgware Rd *YO10*	18	C5
Eighth Av *YO31*	19	E2
Elands Yd **2** *YO1*	5	G5
Elder Gro (Haxby) *YO32*	7	H2
Eldon St *YO31*	18	C1
Eldon Ter *YO31*	18	C1
Eldwick Cl *YO30*	12	A4
Elgar Cl *YO31*	13	F4
Eliot Ct (Fulford) *YO10*	25	H2
Ellwood Ct *YO10*	18	C5
Elma Gro *YO30*	11	H3
Elm End (Haxby) *YO32*	8	A1
Elmfield Av *YO31*	13	G5
Elmfield Ter *YO31*	13	G6
Elm Gro *YO31*	13	G3
Elmlands Gro *YO31*	13	G6
Elmpark Vale *YO31*	13	H6
Elmpark Vw *YO31*	13	H5
Elmpark Way *YO31*	13	H5
Elm Tree Av (U.Pop.) *YO26*	10	C3
Elm Tree Gdns **3** *YO24*	16	D4
Elston Cl *YO30*	12	B5
Elvington La (Dun.) *YO19*	20	D3
Elvington La (Grimston) *YO19*	21	E5
Elvington Ter *YO10*	5	H4
Elwick Gro **3** *YO10*	19	H3
Embleton Dr *YO30*	12	A4
Emerald St *YO31*	18	C1
Emily Ms **7** *YO10*	18	D4
Emmerson St **2** *YO31*	18	D2
Endfields Rd *YO10*	26	A1
Enfield Cres *YO24*	17	G4
Ennerdale Av *YO31*	19	G2
Escrick St *YO10*	5	F6
Escrick Ter **3** *YO10*	5	G6
Eskdale Av *YO10*	19	H4
Esk Dr (N.Pop.) *YO26*	11	E5
Esplanade, The *YO30*	4	A1
Esplanade Ct *YO30*	4	B2
Etive Pl *YO24*	23	H2
Eton Dr (Wig.) *YO32*	7	G1
Etty Av *YO10*	19	F3
Eva Av *YO30*	11	G3
Evelyn Cres *YO30*	12	C6
Exhibition Sq *YO1*	4	D2
Exhibition Sq *YO30*	4	D2
Eye of York *YO1*	5	F5

F

Name		
Faber Cl (Cop.) *YO23*	22	B1
Faber St *YO31*	5	H2
Fairfax Cft (Cop.) *YO23*	22	B2
Fairfax St *YO1*	4	C5
Fairfields Dr (Skel.) *YO30*	6	A6
Fairway *YO30*	12	B5
Fairway Dr (U.Pop.) *YO26*	10	C4
Falcon Cl (Haxby) *YO32*	8	B2
Falconer St *YO24*	17	G4
Falkland St **7** *YO1*	4	D5
Falsgrave Cres *YO30*	12	C6
Farfield *YO30*	16	D1
Farmers Way (Cop.) *YO23*	22	B1
Farmlands Rd *YO24*	24	B1
Farmstead Ri (Haxby) *YO32*	8	A4

Name		
Farndale Av *YO10*	19	H3
Farndale Cl (Haxby) *YO32*	8	B1
Farndale St *YO10*	18	C5
Farrar St *YO10*	18	D4
Farriers Chase (Stren.) *YO32*	9	F6
Farriers Cft **2** (Cop.) *YO23*	22	B1
Fawcett St *YO10*	5	F6
Fawkes Dr *YO26*	16	D3
Feasegate **9** *YO1*	5	E3
Fellbrook Av *YO26*	16	C3
Fenwicks La (Fulford) *YO10*	25	H2
Fenwick St *YO23*	18	B5
Ferguson Way (Hunt.) *YO32*	13	G4
Fern Cl (Hunt.) *YO32*	13	G1
Fern St *YO31*	5	F1
Fernway *YO10*	19	H4
Ferry La (Bish.) *YO23*	25	F5
Ferrymans Wk **1** (N.Pop.) *YO26*	10	C3
Fetter La *YO1*	4	D4
Feversham Cres *YO31*	12	D6
Fewster Way *YO10*	5	F6
Fewston Dr *YO30*	12	A4
Field La *YO10*	19	G5
Field Vw *YO30*	12	D6
Fifth Av *YO31*	5	H1
Filey Ter *YO30*	12	D6
Finkle St *YO1*	5	E3
Finsbury Av *YO23*	18	B6
Finsbury St *YO23*	18	B6
Firbank Cl **4** (Stren.) *YO32*	9	F4
Fir Heath Cl *YO24*	16	D6
First Av *YO31*	19	E1
Firtree Cl (Acomb) *YO24*	17	F4
Fir Tree Cl (Ears.) *YO32*	8	C4
Firwood Whin **1** *YO31*	13	G3
Fishergate *YO10*	5	F5
Fishergate Bar *YO1*	5	G5
Fitzroy Ter *YO10*	5	G6
Flavian Gro *YO30*	12	A5
Flaxman Av *YO10*	19	F3
Flaxman Cft (Cop.) *YO23*	22	B1
Flaxton Rd (Stren.) *YO32*	9	H4
Fleming Av *YO31*	18	D2
Fletcher Ct **1** (Wig.) *YO32*	7	H4
Fletchers Cft **1** (Cop.) *YO23*	22	C1
Florence Gro *YO30*	11	G3
Fold Wk (Stren.) *YO32*	9	H2
Folks Cl (Haxby) *YO32*	8	B2
Fordlands Cres (Fulford) *YO19*	26	A3
Fordlands Rd (Fulford) *YO19*	26	B5
Forest Cl (Wig.) *YO32*	7	G3
Forest Ct **2** (Stren.) *YO32*	9	F4
Foresters Wk *YO24*	16	C6
Forestgate (Haxby) *YO32*	7	H4
Forest Gro *YO31*	19	E1
Forest Way *YO31*	19	E1
Forge Cl (Hunt.) *YO32*	13	G3
Forth St *YO26*	17	G1
Foss Bk *YO31*	5	G2
Foss Br *YO1*	5	F4
Foss Ct *YO31*	13	F4
Fossgate *YO1*	5	F4
Foss Islands Rd *YO31*	5	G3
Fossland Vw (Stren.) *YO32*	9	F4
Foss Wk (N.Pop.) *YO26*	11	E5
Fossway *YO31*	13	F6
Foston Gro *YO31*	13	G5
Foundry La *YO26*	17	G2
Fountayne St *YO31*	12	D6
Fourth Av *YO31*	18	D2
Fox Covert *YO31*	13	G3
Foxcroft (Haxby) *YO32*	7	H5
Fox Garth (N.Pop.) *YO26*	10	D2
Foxthorn Paddock *YO10*	20	A4
Foxton *YO24*	24	A1
Foxwood La *YO24*	23	H1
Frances St *YO10*	18	C6
Frazer Ct *YO30*	11	H5
Frederic St *YO30*	4	B2
Freemans Ct **2** *YO30*	12	B6
Friargate **16** *YO1*	5	E4
Friars Ter **12** *YO1*	5	E5
Friars Wk *YO31*	13	F6
Front St (Acomb) *YO24*	16	D4
Fryers Ct (Murton) *YO19*	20	D2
Fulford Ct *YO10*	25	H4
Fulford Cross *YO10*	18	C6
Fulfordgate *YO10*	26	A2
Fulford Ind Est *YO10*	18	C6

Name	Page	Grid
Fulford Ms (Fulford) YO10	26	A3
Fulford Pk (Fulford) YO10	25	H2
Fulford Rd YO10	18	C6
Furness Dr YO30	11	H4
Furnwood (Haxby) YO32	7	H4
Fylingdales Av YO30	11	H5

G

Name	Page	Grid
Gainsborough Cl (Stren.) YO32	9	H2
Gale Fm Ct YO24	16	D4
Gale La YO24	16	D4
Galligap La YO10	19	H2
Gallops, The YO24	23	H1
Galmanhoe La YO30	4	C1
Galtres Av YO31	14	A6
Galtres Gro YO30	12	A6
Galtres Rd YO31	14	A5
Ganton Ct YO24	24	C2
Garbett Way (Bish.) YO23	25	F6
Garburn Gro YO30	11	H4
Garbutt Gro YO26	17	E2
Gardeners Cl (Cop.) YO23	22	B1
Garden Flats La (Dun.) YO19	21	G1
Garden Pl YO1	5	F3
Garden St YO31	18	B1
Garfield Ter YO26	17	G2
Garlands, The YO26	12	B5
Garnet Ter YO26	17	F2
Garrowby Way (Hes.) YO10	26	D1
Garrow Hill YO10	19	E4
Garrow Hill Av YO10	19	F4
Garth Ct (Hunt.) YO32	13	H1
Garth End (Hunt.) YO32	13	G1
Garth Rd (Hunt.) YO32	13	G1
Garths End YO10	26	A1
Garths End (Haxby) YO32	8	C2
Garth Ter YO30	12	C6
Garth Way (N.Ears.) YO32	13	E2
Gascoigne Wk YO23	4	D6
Gateland Cl (Haxby) YO32	7	H4
Gay Meadows (St.For.) YO32	15	G1
Geldof Rd (Hunt.) YO32	13	G4
George Cayley Dr YO30	12	B2
George Ct YO31	5	F1
George Hudson St YO1	4	C4
George St YO1	5	F5
Gerard Av YO31	19	F2
Giles Av YO31	19	F2
Gillamoor Av 3 YO31	19	G2
Gillingwood Rd YO30	12	A2
Gillygate YO1	4	D1
Girvan Cl YO24	23	H2
Givendale Gro 6 YO10	19	H4
Glade, The YO31	14	A6
Gladstone St (Acomb) YO24	17	E4
Gladstone St YO31	18	C1
Glaisby Ct YO31	19	F1
Glaisdale YO24	24	B2
Glebe, The (Dun.) YO19	21	G1
Glebe Av YO26	17	E2
Glebe Cl (Stren.) YO32	9	G4
Glebe Way (Haxby) YO32	7	H2
Glen Av YO31	5	H1
Glen Cl (Fulford) YO10	26	A3
Glencoe St 9 YO30	12	C6
Glenridding YO24	24	B2
Glen Rd YO31	18	D2
Golands Cotts (Haxby) YO32	8	B1
Goodramgate YO1	5	E3
Goodricke Way (Hes.) YO10	19	F6
Goodwood Gro YO24	17	G6
Gordon St YO10	5	H6
Gormire Av YO31	13	F3
Gorse Hill (Dun.) YO19	21	H1
Gorse Paddock YO31	13	G3
Gouthwaite Cl YO30	12	A3
Government Ho Rd YO30	17	G1
Gower Rd YO24	24	C1
Grampian Cl (Hunt.) YO32	8	C6
Granary Ct 22 YO1	5	E3
Grange Cl (Skel.) YO30	6	A6
Grange Garth YO10	18	C5
Grange La YO23	16	A5
Grange La YO26	16	B5
Granger Av YO26	16	D3
Granger Pl YO26	16	D3
Grange St YO10	18	C5
Grantham Dr YO26	17	F4
Grants Av YO10	26	A1
Granville Ter YO10	18	D4
Grape La 2 YO1	5	E2
Grasmere Dr YO10	19	G3
Grasmere Gro YO30	12	A4
Grassholme YO24	24	A2
Grayshon Dr YO26	16	C2
Gray St YO23	18	A5
Great N Way (N.Pop.) YO26	11	F5
Green, The (Dun.) YO19	21	H2
Green, The (Acomb) YO26	16	D4
Green, The (U.Pop.) YO26	10	C4
Greenacres (Hunt.) YO32	13	G1
Greencliffe Dr YO30	17	H1
Greencroft Ct (Dun.) YO19	21	H1
Greencroft La (Dun.) YO19	21	H2
Green Dike (Wig.) YO32	7	G3
Green Dykes La YO10	19	E4
Greenfield Pk Dr YO31	13	H6
Greengate (A.Bry.) YO23	23	F4
Green La YO23	25	F3
Green La (Acomb) YO24	17	E5
Green La (Clifton) YO30	12	A4
Green La Trd Est (Clifton) YO30	12	B4
Green Meadows YO31	13	H6
Greensborough Av YO26	16	C2
Greenshaw Dr (Haxby) YO32	7	H3
Greenshaw Dr (Wig.) YO32	7	G2
Greenside (Dun.) YO19	21	H2
Greenside Cl (Dun.) YO19	21	H2
Greenside Wk (Dun.) YO19	21	H2
Green Sward YO31	13	H5
Greenway (Hunt.) YO32	13	G1
Greenway, The (Haxby) YO32	7	H4
Greenwich Cl 5 YO30	11	H2
Greenwood Gro YO24	23	H1
Gregory Cl (Skel.) YO30	6	B6
Gresley Ct YO26	16	C3
Greystoke Rd YO30	11	H4
Greystone Ct (Haxby) YO32	7	H5
Grimwith Garth 5 YO30	12	A3
Grosvenor Pk YO30	18	A1
Grosvenor Rd YO30	18	A1
Grosvenor Ter YO30	18	A1
Grove, The YO24	24	C3
Grove Gdns 2 (U.Pop.) YO26	10	C4
Groves Ct YO31	5	F1
Groves La YO31	5	F1
Grove Ter YO24	16	D4
Grove Ter La YO24	18	C1
Grove Vw YO30	17	H1
Guardian Ct YO30	12	B6
Guildhall, The YO1	4	D3

H

Name	Page	Grid
Haddon Cl YO24	16	D5
Hadrian Av YO10	19	G4
Haleys Ter YO31	13	E5
Halifax Ct YO30	12	B4
Halladale Cl YO24	23	H2
Hallard Way (Stren.) YO32	9	G4
Hallcroft La (Cop.) YO23	22	A1
Hallfield Rd YO31	5	H2
Hall Pk (Hes.) YO10	19	G6
Hall Ri (Haxby) YO32	8	A2
Hambleton Av YO10	19	H3
Hambleton Ter YO31	12	D6
Hambleton Vw 10 (Wig.) YO32	7	G1
Hambleton Way (Hunt.) YO32	13	G2
Hamilton Dr YO24	17	F5
Hamilton Dr E YO24	17	G5
Hamilton Dr W YO24	17	E5
Hamilton Way YO24	17	F5
Hammerton Cl YO26	16	C4
Hampden St YO1	4	D5
Handley Cl 3 YO30	12	B3
Hanover St E 6 YO26	17	G2
Hanover St W 4 YO26	17	G2
Hansom Pl 8 YO31	12	D6
Harcourt (Bish.) YO23	25	E6
Harcourt St YO31	18	D2
Harden Cl YO30	12	A3
Hardisty Ms 3 YO26	17	G3
Harewood Cl YO30	11	G3
Harewood Cl (Wig.) YO32	7	G1
Harewood Way (Hes.) YO10	19	F5
Harington Av YO10	19	E3
Harlow Cl YO24	17	G5
Harlow Ct 3 (Stren.) YO32	9	F5
Harlow Rd YO24	17	G5
Harold Ct YO24	17	E4
Harrison St YO31	19	E1
Harrow Glade YO30	12	B4
Hartoft St YO10	18	C5
Harvest Cl (Stren.) YO32	9	G4
Haslemere Cl (Hunt.) YO32	13	F2
Hastings Cl YO30	12	B4
Hatfield Cl 3 YO30	11	H2
Hatfield Wk YO24	23	H1
Hatters Cl 5 (Cop.) YO23	22	B1
Haughton Rd YO30	12	D6
Haverah Ct 8 YO30	12	A4
Hawkshead Cl YO24	23	H1
Hawthorn Cl (N.Ears.) YO32	13	E2
Hawthorne Av (Haxby) YO32	8	A2
Hawthorne Cl (N.Pop.) YO26	10	C3
Hawthorn Gro YO31	5	H1
Hawthorn Meadow 15 YO30	12	B5
Hawthorn Pl 1 (N.Ears.) YO32	13	F1
Hawthorn Spinney YO31	13	F2
Hawthorn St YO31	5	H1
Hawthorn Ter (N.Ears.) YO32	13	E2
Hawthorn Ter Cen (N.Ears.) YO32	13	E2
Hawthorn Ter N (N.Ears.) YO32	13	E1
Hawthorn Ter S (N.Ears.) YO32	13	E2
Haxby Moor Rd (Stren.) YO32	9	F3
Haxby Rd YO31	18	B1
Haxby Rd (N.Ears.) YO32	13	E4
Hayforth Cl 4 YO30	12	B3
Hazel Cl 2 (N.Ears.) YO32	13	E3
Hazel Garth YO31	19	G1
Hazelnut Gro YO30	12	B3
Hazelwood Av YO10	20	A3
Headland Cl (Haxby) YO32	7	H2
Headley Cl YO30	12	B4
Healey Gro YO31	13	G5
Heath Cl YO24	17	G5
Heath Cft YO10	26	B2
Heather Bk YO10	19	H3
Heather Cl (Hunt.) YO32	13	H1
Heather Cft YO31	13	F3
Heathfield Rd YO10	19	F4
Heath Moor Dr YO10	26	B1
Heath Ride (Stren.) YO32	9	H2
Hebden Ri YO26	17	E4
Helmsdale YO24	23	H2
Helmsley Gro (Wig.) YO32	7	F2
Hemlock Av YO31	13	F4
Hempland Av YO31	19	E1
Hempland Dr YO31	13	H6
Hempland La YO31	13	H6
Hendon Garth YO30	12	B4
Herbert St 2 YO10	18	D4
Herberts Way YO31	13	G6
Herdsman Dr (Cop.) YO23	22	C1
Herdsman Rd YO24	24	B1
Herdwick Cl YO30	12	B4
Herman Wk YO24	24	A1
Heron Av YO31	13	G5
Heron Ri (Hunt.) YO32	8	C6
Hesketh Bk YO10	19	H4
Heslin Cl 3 (Haxby) YO32	7	H3
Heslington Ct (Hes.) YO10	19	G6
Heslington Cft (Fulford) YO10	26	A1
Heslington La YO10	26	A2
Heslington Rd YO10	5	H6
Hessay Pl YO26	16	B4
Hetherton St YO30	4	B2
Hewley Av YO10	19	E3
Heworth Grn YO31	5	G1
Heworth Hall Dr YO31	19	E1
Heworth Ms YO31	5	H1
Heworth Pl YO31	19	E1
Heworth Rd YO31	19	E1
Heworth Village YO31	19	E1
Highcliffe YO30	17	H1
High Fld YO10	20	A3
Highgrove Cl 4 YO30	11	H2
Highlands Av (Stren.) YO32	9	G4

Highmoor Cl YO24	24	B1
Highmoor Rd YO24	24	B1
High Newbiggin St 5 YO31	5	E1
High Oaks YO31	14	A6
High Ousegate YO1	5	E4
High Petergate YO1	4	D2
Highthorn Rd YO31	13	F3
Hilbeck Gro YO31	19	G1
Hilbra Av (Haxby) YO32	8	A5
Hilda St YO10	18	D4
Hillary Garth 3 YO26	17	G3
Hillcrest Av (N.Pop.) YO26	10	D3
Hillcrest Gdns YO24	17	G6
Hillsborough Ter 1 YO30	12	D6
Hill St YO24	17	F4
Hill Vw YO31	14	B6
Hinton Av YO24	24	A1
Hobgate YO24	17	E4
Hob Moor Dr YO24	17	F5
Hob Moor Ter YO24	17	G6
Hobson Cl (Cop.) YO23	22	A3
Hodgson La (U.Pop.) YO26	10	B5
Holburns (Hes.) YO10	19	F6
Holgate Br Gdns 2 YO24	17	H4
Holgate Lo Dr YO26	17	F3
Holgate Rd YO24	17	G4
Hollands Rd YO10	18	D6
Hollis Cres (Stren.) YO32	9	G5
Holly Bk Gro YO24	17	G5
Holly Bk Rd YO24	17	G5
Holly Ter 5 YO10	18	C6
Holly Tree Cft (Dun.) YO19	21	H1
Holly Tree La (Dun.) YO19	21	H1
Holly Tree La (Haxby) YO32	8	A3
Holmefield La YO10	19	F6
Holroyd Av YO31	19	F2
Holtby La (Holtby) YO19	15	E3
Holyrood Dr YO30	11	G2
Homefield Cl (Cop.) YO23	22	A2
Homestead Cl (Hunt.) YO32	13	G4
Hope St YO10	5	G5
Hopgrove La N YO32	14	B2
Hopgrove La S YO32	14	C2
Hornbeam Cl YO30	12	C3
Horner St YO30	12	C6
Hornsey Garth (Wig.) YO32	7	H2
Horseman Av (Cop.) YO23	22	A1
Horseman Cl (Cop.) YO23	22	A1
Horseman Dr (Cop.) YO23	22	A1
Horseman La (Cop.) YO23	22	A1
Horseshoe, The YO24	24	C2
Horsfield Way (Dun.) YO19	21	H1
Horsman Av YO10	5	G6
Hospital Flds 6 YO10	18	C6
Hospital Flds Rd YO10	18	B6
Hospital La YO31	18	B1
Hotham Av YO30	16	C5
Hothams Ct YO1	5	F4
Houndsway YO24	23	H1
Howard Dr YO30	11	G3
Howard Link YO30	11	G3
Howard Rd (Stren.) YO32	9	G5
Howard St YO10	18	C5
Howe Hill Cl YO26	17	F3
Howe Hill Rd YO26	17	F3
Howe St 5 YO24	17	E4
Hubert St YO23	18	A6
Huby Ct 1 YO1	5	H5
Hudson Cres 4 YO30	12	B6
Hudson St 3 YO30	12	D6
Hudson Way (N.Pop.) YO26	11	F5
Hull Rd YO10	19	F4
Hull Rd (Dun.) YO19	21	E3
Humber Dr (Stren.) YO32	9	G5
Hungate YO1	5	F3
Hunt Ct YO1	5	F2
Hunters Cl (Dun.) YO19	21	F2
Hunters Cl 6 (Haxby) YO32	7	H3
Hunters Way YO24	24	D2
Hunterswood Way (Dun.) YO19	21	G2
Huntington Ms YO31	13	E6
Huntington Rd YO31	13	E6
Huntington Rd (Hunt.) YO32	13	F3
Huntsmans Wk YO24	16	D6
Hurricane Way YO30	11	H2
Hursts Yd YO1	5	G4
Hutton Cl (N.Pop.) YO26	10	D3
Hyrst Gro YO31	18	D1

I

Ikin Way (Hunt.) YO32	8	C6
Ilton Garth YO30	12	B3
Ingleborough Av YO10	19	G3
Ingleton Wk YO31	19	F2
Ingram Av YO30	12	C5
Ings La (N.Pop.) YO26	11	E4
Ings Vw YO30	11	G3
Ings Way YO30	12	A5
Inman Ter YO26	17	E3
Innovation Way (Hes.) YO10	19	G5
Intake Av YO30	12	D6
Intake La (Dun.) YO19	21	H2
Invicta Ct YO24	23	H1
Irvine Way YO24	23	H2
Irwin Av YO31	18	D1
Iver Cl YO26	16	D2
Ivy Pl (N.Ears.) YO32	13	E2

J

Jackson St YO31	18	C1
Jacobi Cl YO30	12	B6
James Backhouse Pl YO24	17	F4
James Nicholson Link YO30	12	B3
James St YO10	5	H3
James Way (Hes.) YO10	19	F6
Jamieson Ter YO23	18	A6
Jasmine Cl (N.Ears.) YO32	13	E3
Jaywick Cl (Stren.) YO32	9	H2
Jedwell Cl 2 (N.Ears.) YO32	13	E1
Jennifer Gro YO24	17	G5
Jervis Rd YO24	24	B1
Jewbury YO31	5	F2
Jockey La (Hunt.) YO32	14	A4
John St YO31	18	D1
Jorvik Cl YO26	16	D2
Jubbergate YO1	5	E3
Jubilee Ct (Haxby) YO32	8	A3
Jubilee Ter YO26	17	G2
Judges Ct 10 YO1	4	D3
Julia Av (Hunt.) YO32	14	A3
Juniper Cl (N.Ears.) YO32	13	E3
Jute Rd YO26	16	C2

K

Kathryn Av (Hunt.) YO32	13	H3
Keats Cl 1 YO30	12	A5
Keble Cl (Bish.) YO23	25	F6
Keble Dr (Bish.) YO23	25	E6
Keble Pk Cres (Bish.) YO23	25	E6
Keble Pk N (Bish.) YO23	25	E6
Keble Pk S (Bish.) YO23	25	E6
Keeper's Way (Dun.) YO19	21	H1
Keith Av (Hunt.) YO32	13	H1
Keldale (Haxby) YO32	8	B1
Kempton Cl YO24	17	E6
Kendal Cl (Dun.) YO19	21	H1
Kendrew Cl (Hunt.) YO32	13	G2
Kenlay Cl 8 (N.Ears.) YO32	13	E1
Kennedy Dr (Haxby) YO32	8	A2
Kenrick Pl YO26	16	C2
Kensal Ri YO10	18	C5
Kensington Cl (Drin.) YO24	24	D1
Kensington Rd YO30	11	G3
Kensington St YO23	18	A6
Kentmere Dr YO30	11	H4
Kent St YO10	5	G6
Kerrside 6 YO30	11	H5
Kestrel Wd Way YO31	13	F3
Keswick Way (Hunt.) YO32	8	C6
Kettlestring La YO30	12	B3
Kexby Av YO10	19	E4
Key Way (Fulford) YO19	26	A4
Kilburn Rd YO10	18	C5
Kimberlows Wds Hill YO10	19	H4
Kinbrace Dr YO24	23	H2
Kingfisher Cl (Hunt.) YO32	8	C6
Kings Acre YO31	19	G1
Kingsclere (Hunt.) YO32	8	C6
Kings Ct 5 YO1	5	E3
Kingsland Ter YO26	17	G2
Kingsmoor Rd (St.For.) YO32	15	F1
Kings Sq 4 YO1	5	E3
Kings Staith YO1	5	E4
Kingsthorpe YO24	17	E5
King St 18 YO1	5	E4
Kingsway N YO30	12	C6
Kingsway W YO24	17	E5
Kingswood Gro YO24	17	E4
Kir Cres YO24	16	D5
Kirkcroft (Wig.) YO32	7	H3
Kirkdale Rd YO10	20	A3
Kirkham Av YO31	13	E5
Kirklands (Stren.) YO32	9	G4
Kirkstone Dr YO31	19	F1
Kirk Vw YO26	16	D4
Kirkwell (Bish.) YO23	25	E5
Kitchener St YO31	13	E6
Kitemere Pl YO24	23	H1
Knapton Cl (Stren.) YO32	9	G5
Knapton La YO26	16	C3
Knavesmire Cres YO23	18	A6
Knavesmire Rd YO23	17	H5
Knoll, The YO24	16	C6
Kyle Way (N.Pop.) YO26	11	E5
Kyme St YO1	4	D5

L

Laburnum Garth YO31	13	G5
Lady Hamilton Gdns YO24	17	E5
Lady Hewley's Cotts 3 YO1	5	F3
Lady Mill Garth 6 YO30	12	C5
Lady Peckitts Yd 13 YO1	5	E4
Lady Rd YO30	12	C6
Ladysmith Ms 5 (Stren.) YO32	9	F4
Lady Wortley Pl (Midd.) YO23	25	G3
Lakeside Ct 1 YO24	24	D1
Lakeside Gdns (Stren.) YO32	9	H2
Lambert Ct 1 YO4	4	D5
Lamel St YO10	19	F4
Lamplugh Cres (Bish.) YO23	25	F6
Lancar Cl (Wig.) YO32	7	F2
Lancaster Way YO30	12	B4
Landalewood Rd 3 YO30	12	A3
Landau Cl 4 YO30	12	A5
Landing La YO26	17	F2
Landing La (Haxby) YO32	8	C2
Landings, The (Haxby) YO32	8	B2
Landsdown Way (Haxby) YO32	8	B2
Lang Av YO10	19	F3
Langdale Av YO31	19	F1
Langholme Dr YO26	16	D1
Langley Ct (Hunt.) YO32	8	C6
Lang Rd (Bish.) YO23	24	D5
Lang Rd (Hunt.) YO32	8	C6
Langsett Gro YO30	12	A2
Langton Ct (Stren.) YO32	9	F5
Langwith La (Hes.) YO10	27	G2
Lansdowne Ter YO10	18	D4
Lanshaw Cft YO32	12	A4
Larchfield YO31	14	A6
Larch Way (Haxby) YO32	8	A1
Larkfield Cl (Cop.) YO23	22	A1
Lasenby Cl 1 (N.Ears.) YO32	13	E1
Lastingham Ter YO10	18	C5
Lavender Gro YO26	17	F2
Lawnswood Dr YO30	12	A5
Lawnway YO31	13	H6
Lawrence Ct YO10	5	H5
Lawrence St YO10	5	H5
Lawson Rd YO24	24	D3
Layerthorpe YO31	5	G2
Layerthorpe Br YO31	5	G2
Leadley Cft (Cop.) YO23	22	A3
Lead Mill La YO1	5	F5
Leake St YO10	5	H5
Learmans Way (Cop.) YO23	22	C1
Lea Way (Hunt.) YO32	13	H1
Leeman Rd YO26	4	A3
Leeside YO24	24	B1
Leicester Way 6 YO1	5	F5
Leighton Cft YO30	12	A4
Lendal YO1	4	D3
Lendal Br YO1	4	D3
Lerecroft Rd YO24	24	B1
Lesley Av YO10	26	A1
Leven Rd YO24	24	B2
Levisham St YO10	18	C5
Leyes, The YO10	19	H3
Leyfield Cl 1 (Stren.) YO32	9	F4

Name		
Leyland Rd YO31	19	F2
Library Sq 7 YO1	4	D2
Lichfield Ct YO23	18	A6
Lidgett Gro YO26	16	C1
Lilac Av YO10	19	G4
Lilbourne Dr YO30	12	B5
Lilling Av YO31	13	F5
Lime Av YO31	13	G6
Lime Garth (U.Pop.) YO26	10	C4
Limes, The (St.For.) YO32	15	F1
Limes Ct YO31	19	E1
Lime Tree Av (N.Ears.) YO32	13	E2
Lime Tree Ms (Dun.) YO19	21	H1
Lincoln St YO26	17	G2
Lindale YO24	24	A2
Linden Cl (Hunt.) YO32	8	C6
Linden Gro YO30	12	A5
Lindley Rd YO30	12	A4
Lindley St YO24	17	G4
Lindley Wd Gro 7 YO30	11	H2
Lindsey Av YO26	17	E3
Lingfield Cres YO24	17	G6
Link, The YO10	26	A1
Link, The (Cop.) YO23	22	A1
Link Av YO30	12	D5
Link Business Pk (Osb.) YO10	20	A3
Link Rd YO32	13	E3
Link Rd Ct (Osb.) YO10	20	A3
Linley Av (Haxby) YO32	8	B2
Linnet Way YO24	24	A1
Linton (N.Pop.) YO26	10	D4
Linton St YO26	17	F2
Lister Way YO30	12	B6
Little Av YO30	12	C5
Littlefield Cl (N.Pop.) YO26	10	C3
Little Garth (N.Pop.) YO26	10	C3
Little Hallfield Rd YO31	5	H2
Little La (Haxby) YO32	8	A2
Little Meadows (Haxby) YO32	8	A3
Little Shambles YO1	5	E3
Little Stonegate YO1	4	D3
Livingstone St YO26	17	G2
Lloyd Cl (Hes.) YO10	19	G6
Lochrin Pl YO26	16	C3
Lockey Cft (Wig.) YO32	7	H3
Lock Ho La (Ears.) YO32	8	C3
Lockwood St YO31	5	F1
Long Cl La YO10	5	G5
Longcroft (Wig.) YO32	7	H1
Longfield Ter YO30	4	B2
Long Furrow (Haxby) YO32	7	H3
Long Ridge Dr (U.Pop.) YO26	10	D4
Long Ridge La YO26	10	C4
Longwood Link YO30	11	H2
Longwood Rd YO30	12	A2
Lord Mayors Wk YO31	5	E1
Lords Moor La (Stren.) YO32	9	H3
Loriners Dr (Cop.) YO23	22	B1
Lorne St YO23	18	A6
Lorrenger La (A.Bry.) YO23	23	F2
Love La YO10	5	G1
Love La YO10	17	H5
Lovel Ho YO24	24	B1
Lovell St YO23	18	B5
Lowcroft (Stren.) YO32	9	F4
Lower Darnborough St YO23	5	E6
Lower Ebor St YO23	18	B5
Lower Friargate 17 YO1	5	E4
Lower Priory St YO1	4	C5
Loweswater Rd 11 YO30	11	H4
Lowfield Dr (Haxby) YO32	8	A1
Lowfield La (Knapton) YO26	16	A3
Low Flds Dr YO24	16	D5
Low Grn (Cop.) YO23	22	B2
Lowick YO24	24	A2
Low La (Hes.) YO10	26	D1
Low Mill Cl YO10	20	A4
Low Moor Av YO10	26	B2
Lown Hill YO24	16	D5
Low Ousegate YO1	4	D4
Low Petergate YO1	5	E2
Low Poppleton La YO26	11	E6
Lowther St YO31	18	B1
Lowther Ter YO24	4	A5
Loxley Cl YO30	12	A3
Lucas Av YO30	12	D5
Lucombe Way (N.Ears.) YO32	13	E1
Lumley Rd YO30	12	C6
Lund Cl (Wig.) YO32	7	G3
Lundy Cl 2 YO30	12	B4
Lycett Rd YO24	24	D3
Lydham Ct YO24	24	A1
Lyndale Av YO10	19	H4
Lynden Way YO24	17	E4
Lynwood Av (Cop.) YO23	22	A1
Lynwood Cl (Stren.) YO32	9	F4
Lynwood Vw (Cop.) YO23	22	A1
Lysander Cl YO30	12	B3

M

Name		
McHugh Ct 1 (Hes.) YO10	26	D1
Maclagan Rd (Bish.) YO23	24	D5
Magnolia Gro 3 (N.Ears.) YO32	13	E3
Maida Gro YO10	18	C5
Main Av YO31	19	E2
Main St (Fulford) YO10	25	H2
Main St (Hes.) YO10	19	F6
Main St (A.Bry.) YO23	22	D4
Main St (A.Rich.) YO23	22	B5
Main St (Bish.) YO23	25	E5
Main St (Cop.) YO23	22	A2
Main St (Knapton) YO26	16	B2
Main St (N.Pop.) YO26	10	B3
Main St (U.Pop.) YO26	10	C3
Malbys Gro (Cop.) YO23	22	B2
Malham Gro YO31	19	G2
Mallard Way (Haxby) YO32	8	B2
Mallory Cl 6 (N.Ears.) YO32	13	E1
Malton Av YO31	18	D1
Malton Rd YO31	13	G5
Malton Rd YO32	14	A4
Malton Way YO30	12	A5
Malt Shovel Ct 9 YO1	5	F4
Malvern Av YO26	17	E3
Malvern Cl (Hunt.) YO32	8	D6
Mancroft (Haxby) YO32	7	H4
Manley Cl 7 (N.Ears.) YO32	13	E1
Manor Beeches, The (Dun.) YO19	21	G1
Manor Cl (U.Pop.) YO26	10	C5
Manor Ct (U.Pop.) YO26	10	C5
Manor Ct 1 (Hunt.) YO32	8	C5
Manor Dr (Dun.) YO19	21	G2
Manor Dr N YO26	17	E3
Manor Dr S YO26	17	E3
Manor Fm Cl (Cop.) YO23	22	A2
Manor Garth (Wig.) YO32	7	G3
Manor Heath (Cop.) YO23	22	A1
Manor La YO30	11	G3
Manor Pk Cl YO30	11	H3
Manor Pk Gro YO30	11	G3
Manor Pk Rd YO30	11	G3
Manor Way YO30	11	H3
Mansfield St YO31	5	G2
Manthorpe Wk YO26	17	F3
Maple Av (Bish.) YO23	25	E6
Maple Ct (N.Ears.) YO32	13	E2
Maple Gro YO10	18	C6
Maplehurst Av YO31	13	E6
Maplewood Paddock YO24	16	D6
March St YO31	18	C1
Margaret Philipson Ct 2 YO1	5	F2
Margaret St YO10	5	G5
Marjorie Waite Ct 5 YO30	12	C6
Market St YO1	5	E4
Markham Cres YO31	18	B1
Markham St YO31	18	B1
Marlborough Cl 1 YO30	11	G2
Marlborough Gro YO10	18	C5
Marlborough Vil 8 YO10	18	C5
Marmian Dr (St.For.) YO32	15	F1
Marsden Pk YO32	12	B3
Marston Av YO26	16	C4
Marston Cres YO26	16	C4
Marten Cl 11 YO30	12	B5
Martin Cheeseman Ct YO24	24	A1
Martin's Ct YO26	17	H2
Marygate YO30	4	C2
Marygate La YO30	4	C2
Matmer Ct YO10	19	E4
Mattison Way YO24	17	F5
Mayfield Gro YO24	24	D1
Maythorn Rd YO31	13	F3
Meadlands YO31	19	G1
Meadowbeck Cl YO10	19	G3
Meadow Ct YO24	24	C1
Meadowfields Dr YO31	13	E3
Meadow La (Haxby) YO32	8	A3
Meadows, The 1 (Skel.) YO30	6	A6
Meadow Way YO31	13	G6
Meadow Way (Hunt.) YO32	13	G1
Meam Cl YO10	20	A3
Melander Cl YO26	16	C3
Melander Gdns (Haxby) YO32	8	A4
Melbourne St YO10	18	C5
Melcombe Av (Stren.) YO32	9	G4
Melrose Cl YO31	19	F2
Melrose Ct YO31	19	E3
Melrosegate YO10	19	E4
Melrosegate YO31	19	E2
Melroses Yd YO1	5	G4
Melton Av YO30	12	A5
Melton Dr (Bish.) YO23	25	E6
Melton Dr YO30	12	A5
Melwood Gro YO26	16	C2
Mendip Cl (Hunt.) YO32	8	C6
Merchant Gate YO1	5	F4
Merchant Way (Cop.) YO23	22	B1
Merlin Covert 5 YO31	13	G2
Metcalfe La (Osb.) YO19	19	H2
Micklegate YO1	4	C4
Micklegate Bar YO1	4	B5
Middle Banks (Wig.) YO32	7	G2
Middlecroft Dr (Stren.) YO32	9	F4
Middlecroft Gro (Stren.) YO32	9	G4
Middleham Av YO31	13	F5
Middlethorpe Dr YO24	24	C2
Middlethorpe Gro YO24	24	D2
Middleton Rd YO24	17	E5
Midway Av (N.Pop.) YO26	10	D4
Mildred Gro YO24	17	G5
Milford Way (Haxby) YO32	8	A4
Millers Cft (Cop.) YO23	22	B1
Millfield Av YO10	19	E4
Millfield Gdns (N.Pop.) YO26	10	D3
Millfield La YO10	19	F4
Millfield La (N.Pop.) YO26	11	E5
Millfield Rd YO23	18	A5
Mill Gates YO26	16	D1
Mill Hill Dr (Hunt.) YO32	13	G1
Mill La (A.Bry.) YO23	23	F5
Mill La YO31	18	D1
Mill La (Wig.) YO32	7	F2
Mill Mt YO24	4	A6
Mill Mt Ct YO24	4	A6
Mill St YO1	5	F5
Milner St YO24	17	E4
Milson Gro YO10	19	F4
Milton Carr YO30	12	A4
Milton St YO10	19	E4
Minchin Cl YO30	12	C5
Minster Av YO31	13	G3
Minster Cl (Wig.) YO32	7	H2
Minster Ct 8 YO1	5	E1
Minster Gates 1 YO1	5	E2
Minster Vw (Wig.) YO32	7	H3
Minster Yd YO1	5	E2
Minter Cl YO24	16	C6
Mistral Ct YO31	13	E6
Mitchell Way YO30	11	H2
Mitchels La YO10	26	B1
Miterdale YO24	24	A2
Moat Fld YO10	19	H3
Moatside Ct YO31	5	E1
Moins Ct YO10	20	A3
Moiser Cl 10 (N.Ears.) YO32	13	E1
Monk Av YO31	13	G6
Monk Bar Ct 1 YO1	5	F2
Monk Br YO31	18	C1
Monkgate YO31	5	F1
Monkgate Cloisters YO31	5	F1
Monks Cross Dr (Hunt.) YO32	13	H2
Monks Cross Link YO32	9	E6
Monkton Rd YO31	13	F5
Montague Gdns (Bish.) YO23	25	E6
Montague St YO23	18	A6
Montague Wk (U.Pop.) YO26	10	C3
Montrose Av YO31	13	E5
Moorcroft Rd YO24	24	B3
Moore Av YO24	19	G3
Moorgarth Av YO24	17	G5
Moorgate YO24	24	C1
Moor Gro YO24	24	C1
Moorland Gdns (Cop.) YO23	22	A3

Name	Page	Grid
Moorland Garth (Stren.) YO32	9	F3
Moorland Rd YO10	25	H1
Moorlands Cl YO10	19	H3
Moorlands Flds YO10	26	A1
Moorlands Rd (Skel.) YO30	6	B5
Moor La (Murton) YO19	20	C1
Moor La (A.Bry.) YO23	23	H3
Moor La (Bish.) YO23	24	D6
Moor La (Cop.) YO23	22	A3
Moor La YO24	24	C2
Moor La (Haxby) YO32	7	H1
Moor La (Stren.) YO32	9	G4
Moor Lea Av YO24	24	C1
Moor Way (Hunt.) YO32	13	H1
Morehall Cl YO30	12	A3
Morrell Ct YO24	23	H1
Morritt Cl YO31	13	G4
Moss St YO23	4	B6
Mount, The YO24	4	A6
Mount Ephraim YO24	4	A5
Mount Par YO24	4	A6
Mount Vale YO24	17	H5
Mount Vale Dr YO24	17	H5
Mowbray Dr YO26	16	D3
Muirfield Way YO26	16	C2
Mulberry Ct (Hunt.) YO32	8	C5
Mulberry Dr (Haxby) YO32	8	A1
Mulwith Cl YO31	19	F1
Muncastergate YO31	13	F6
Murray St YO24	17	G4
Murrough Wilson Pl YO31	12	D6
Murton Garth (Murton) YO19	20	C1
Murton La (Murton) YO19	20	C1
Murton Way YO19	20	B2
Museum St YO1	4	C3
Myrtle Av (Bish.) YO23	25	F6

N

Name	Page	Grid
Naburn La (Fulford) YO19	25	G5
Nairn Cl YO24	24	A3
Nalton Cl (Cop.) YO23	22	A3
Navigation Rd YO1	5	G4
Nelsons La YO24	17	G6
Nelson St YO31	18	C1
Nessgate YO1	5	E4
Nether Hornpot La 21 YO1	5	E3
Nether Way (N.Pop.) YO26	10	C3
Nether Way (U.Pop.) YO26	10	C3
Netherwindings (Haxby) YO32	8	C2
Netherwoods (Stren.) YO32	9	G3
Neville Dr (Bish.) YO23	25	E6
Neville St YO31	18	C1
Neville Ter YO31	18	C1
Nevinson Gro YO10	26	B1
Nevis Way YO24	23	H2
Newborough St YO30	18	A1
Newbury Av YO24	17	E6
Newby Ter 4 YO31	12	D6
Newdale (Haxby) YO32	8	B1
New Forge Ct (Haxby) YO32	8	C2
Newgate 7 YO1	5	E3
Newland Pk Cl YO10	19	E4
Newland Pk Dr YO10	19	F4
Newlands Dr YO26	16	C1
Newlands Rd (Bish.) YO23	24	D5
New La (Bish.) YO23	24	D5
New La YO24	17	F4
New La (Hunt.) YO32	13	G3
New St YO1	4	D3
Newton Ter YO1	4	D5
Newton Way (Stren.) YO32	9	G5
New Wk YO10	5	E6
New Wk Ter YO10	18	C5
Nicholas Gdns YO10	19	E4
Nicholas St YO10	18	D4
Nidd Cl (N.Pop.) YO26	11	E5
Nidd Gro YO24	24	C1
Nigel Gro YO24	17	G5
Nightingale Cl (Hunt.) YO32	13	F4
Ninth Av YO31	19	E2
Norfolk St YO23	18	B5
Norman Dr YO26	16	C1
Norman St 5 YO10	19	F4
Northcote Av YO24	17	F4
Northcroft (Haxby) YO32	8	B2
North Eastern Ter YO24	24	D1
Northfield La (A.Bry.) YO23	23	E3

Name	Page	Grid
Northfield La (U.Pop.) YO26	16	A1
Northfields (Stren.) YO32	9	H2
Northfield Ter YO24	24	C1
Northlands Av 1 (Ears.) YO23	8	C4
North La (Haxby) YO32	8	A2
North La (Hunt.) YO32	8	C6
North Moor (Hunt.) YO32	13	H1
North Moor Gdns (Hunt.) YO32	13	G1
North Moor Rd (Hunt.) YO32	8	C6
Northolme Dr YO30	11	H5
North Par YO30	4	B1
North St YO1	4	D4
Norway Dr YO10	25	H1
Nunmill St YO23	18	B5
Nunnery La YO23	4	B5
Nunthorpe Av YO23	18	A5
Nunthorpe Cres YO23	18	A6
Nunthorpe Dr YO23	18	B5
Nunthorpe Gdns YO23	18	B5
Nunthorpe Gro YO23	18	A6
Nunthorpe Rd YO23	4	C6
Nunthorpe Vw YO23	18	B6
Nursery Ct (N.Pop.) YO26	10	D3
Nursery Dr YO24	17	F4
Nursery Gdns YO10	19	H4
Nursery Rd (N.Pop.) YO26	10	D4

O

Name	Page	Grid
Oakdale Rd YO30	12	A3
Oaken Gro (Haxby) YO32	8	A1
Oak Glade YO31	13	G3
Oakhill Cres (Stren.) YO32	9	F5
Oakland Av YO31	13	G6
Oakland Dr YO31	13	H6
Oaklands (Stren.) YO32	9	G4
Oak Ri YO24	16	D4
Oak St YO26	17	F2
Oak Tree Cl (Stren.) YO32	9	G5
Oak Tree Ct (Haxby) YO32	7	H4
Oak Tree Gro (N.Ears.) YO32	13	E3
Oak Tree La (Haxby) YO32	7	H4
Oak Tree Way (Stren.) YO32	9	G5
Oakville St YO31	13	E6
Ogleforth YO1	5	E2
Ogleforth Ms YO1	5	E1
Old Coppice (Haxby) YO32	8	C2
Old Dike Lands (Haxby) YO32	7	H3
Old Highway, The 3 (Stren.) YO32	9	G5
Oldman Ct YO24	24	A1
Old Moor La YO24	24	C2
Old Orchard (Haxby) YO32	8	A3
Old Orchard, The (Fulford) YO10	26	A2
Old Sch Ct 4 (U.Pop.) YO26	10	C4
Old Village, The (Hunt.) YO32	8	C6
Olympian Ct YO10	19	E4
Orchard, The (Bish.) YO23	25	E6
Orchard Cl YO24	17	F6
Orchard Cotts 1 (Dun.) YO19	21	H1
Orchard Gdns YO31	13	F3
Orchard Garth (Cop.) YO23	22	B1
Orchard Paddock (Haxby) YO32	8	A3
Orchard Rd (U.Pop.) YO26	10	C4
Orchard Vw (Skel.) YO30	6	A6
Orchard Way YO24	24	C1
Orchard Way (Stren.) YO32	9	G3
Ordnance La YO10	18	C6
Oriel Gro YO30	12	B5
Orrin Cl YO24	24	A2
Osbaldwick La YO10	19	G3
Osbaldwick Link Rd YO10	20	A3
Osbaldwick Link Rd YO19	20	A3
Osbaldwick Village YO10	19	H3
Osbourne Dr 6 YO30	11	H2
Osmington Gdns 6 (Stren.) YO32	9	F4
Osprey Cl YO24	23	H1
Ostlers Cl 2 (Cop.) YO23	22	C1
Ostman Rd 3 YO26	16	C2
Otterwood Bk YO24	16	C6
Otterwood La YO24	16	C6
Ouse Acres YO26	17	E2
Ouse Br YO1	4	D4
Ouseburn Av YO26	16	C1

Name	Page	Grid
Ousecliffe Gdns YO30	17	H1
Ouse Lea YO30	12	B6
Ouse Moor La (N.Pop.) YO26	10	B3
Outgang, The (Hes.) YO10	26	D1
Outgang La (Osb.) YO19	20	A2
Overdale Cl YO24	24	B1
Ovington Ter YO23	18	A5
Owlwood Ct (Dun.) YO19	21	G2
Owlwood La (Dun.) YO19	21	G2
Owston Av YO10	19	F4
Ox Calder Cl (Dun.) YO19	21	H2
Ox Carr La (Stren.) YO32	9	G5
Oxclose La (Hes.) YO10	27	G1
Oxford St YO24	4	A5

P

Name	Page	Grid
Paddock, The YO26	16	D1
Paddock, The (Stren.) YO32	9	H3
Paddock Cl (A.Rich.) YO23	22	A4
Paddock Cl (Cop.) YO23	22	A2
Paddock Way YO26	16	D1
Palace Vw (Fulford) YO10	25	H3
Palmer La YO1	5	F3
Parade Ct YO31	19	E1
Paragon St YO1	5	G6
Park Av (N.Ears.) YO32	8	A6
Park Cl (Skel.) YO30	11	E1
Park Ct YO31	19	F2
Park Cres YO31	18	C1
Parker Av YO26	16	C5
Park Est (Haxby) YO32	8	A3
Park Gate (Stren.) YO32	9	H2
Park Gro YO31	18	C1
Parkland Way (Haxby) YO32	8	A3
Park La (Holgate) YO24	17	G4
Parkside Cl YO24	17	F4
Park St YO24	4	B6
Parliament St YO1	5	E3
Paston Wk YO23	4	D6
Pasture Cl (Skel.) YO30	6	A6
Pasture Cl (Stren.) YO32	9	G5
Pasture Fm Cl (Fulford) YO10	25	H3
Pasture La YO32	14	A5
Pastures, The YO24	24	C1
Pately Pl YO26	17	E3
Patrick Pool 6 YO1	5	E3
Patterdale Dr YO30	11	H4
Pavement YO1	5	E4
Paver La YO1	5	G4
Pear Tree Av (U.Pop.) YO26	10	C3
Pear Tree Cl (Hunt.) YO32	13	G1
Pear Tree Ct 5 YO1	5	F2
Pear Tree La (Dun.) YO19	21	G2
Peasholme Grn YO1	5	F3
Peckitt St YO1	5	E5
Peel Cl (Hes.) YO10	19	F6
Peel St YO1	5	G5
Pelham Pl (Stren.) YO32	9	F5
Pembroke St YO30	12	C6
Penleys Ct 8 YO31	18	C1
Penleys Gro St YO31	18	C1
Pennine Cl (Hunt.) YO32	13	G1
Penny La Ct 4 YO1	5	F2
Pentire Cl 1 YO30	12	B4
Pentland Dr (Hunt.) YO32	13	G1
Penyghent Av YO31	19	F2
Peppercorn Cl 1 YO26	17	F3
Percys La YO1	5	G4
Petercroft Cl (Dun.) YO19	21	H1
Petercroft La (Dun.) YO19	21	H1
Peter Hill Dr YO30	12	B5
Peter La YO1	5	E4
Petersway YO30	18	A1
Pheasant Dr YO24	23	H2
Philadelphia Ter YO23	18	A5
Phoenix Boul YO26	17	H3
Piccadilly YO1	5	F4
Pike Hills Mt (Cop.) YO23	22	A1
Pilgrim St 2 YO31	18	B1
Pinelands (Haxby) YO32	8	A4
Pinelands Way YO10	19	H4
Pinewood Gro 3 YO31	13	F4
Pinewood Hill YO10	19	H4
Pinfold Ct 3 YO30	18	B6
Pinsent Ct YO31	13	F5
Plantation Dr YO26	16	D1
Plantation Gro YO26	16	D1

Plantation Way (Wig.) YO32	7	G2
Ploughlands (Haxby) YO32	7	H4
Ploughmans Cl (Cop.) YO23	22	B1
Ploughman's La (Haxby) YO32	7	H4
Plumer Av YO31	19	F2
Pollard Cl (Hunt.) YO32	13	F2
Poplar Gro (N.Ears.) YO32	13	E2
Poplars Cl (St.For.) YO32	15	F1
Poplar St YO26	17	F2
Poppleton Hall Gdns (N.Pop.) YO26	10	D2
Poppleton Rd YO24	17	F3
Poppleton Rd YO26	17	F3
Portal Rd YO26	16	C1
Portisham Pl (Stren.) YO32	9	F4
Portland St YO31	4	D1
Postern Cl YO23	5	E6
Potters Dr 4 (Cop.) YO23	22	B1
Pottery La YO31	13	F6
Precentors Ct YO1	4	D2
Prestwick St YO26	16	C2
Prices La YO32	4	D6
Price St 2 YO23	4	C6
Princess Rd (Stren.) YO32	9	G3
Priors Wk YO26	17	E1
Priory St YO1	4	C5
Priory Wd Way YO31	13	G3
Prospect Ter YO1	4	C5
Prospect Ter (Fulford) YO10	25	H3
Pulleyn Dr YO24	17	G6
Pump Ct 23 YO1	5	E3

Q

Quaker Grn YO24	24	A2
Quant Ms YO10	19	G4
Queen Annes Rd YO30	4	B1
Queens Staith 19 YO1	4	D4
Queens Staith Ms 8 YO1	4	D5
Queens Staith 20 YO1	4	D4
Queen St YO24	4	B4
Queenswood Gro YO24	17	E5
Queen Victoria St YO23	18	A6

R

Radley Ct 2 (Stren.) YO32	9	F5
Railway Ter YO24	17	H3
Railway Vw YO24	24	C1
Rainsborough Way YO30	12	B5
Ramsay Cl YO31	18	C1
Ramsey Av (Bish.) YO23	25	E6
Ratcliffe Ct (Skel.) YO30	6	B6
Ratcliffe St YO30	12	C6
Raven Gro YO26	16	D3
Rawcliffe Av YO30	12	A5
Rawcliffe Cl YO30	11	H3
Rawcliffe Cft YO30	11	G3
Rawcliffe Dr YO30	12	A5
Rawcliffe Gro YO30	12	A6
Rawcliffe Landing (Skel.) YO30	11	F2
Rawcliffe La YO30	12	A5
Rawcliffe Village YO30	11	H2
Rawcliffe Way YO30	11	H3
Rawdon Av YO10	19	E3
Raynard Ct YO24	24	A1
Rectory Gdns YO23	18	A6
Redbarn Dr YO10	20	A4
Redcoat Way YO24	23	H1
Redeness St YO31	5	H2
Redgrave St YO31	13	F5
Redman Cl YO10	25	H1
Redmayne Sq 1 (Stren.) YO32	9	H2
Redmires Cl YO30	12	B3
Redthorn Dr YO31	13	G4
Redwood Dr (Haxby) YO32	7	H2
Reeves, The YO24	16	D6
Regency Ms (Drin.) YO24	24	D1
Regents Ct 11 YO26	17	G2
Regent St YO10	5	H6
Reginald Gro YO23	18	B6
Reighton Av YO30	12	A5
Reighton Dr YO30	12	A4
Renfrew St (Stren.) YO32	9	H2
Renshaw Gdns YO26	17	F3
Reygate Gro (Cop.) YO23	22	B2
Ribstone Gro YO31	19	G1
Richardson St YO23	18	B5
Richmond St YO31	5	H2
Ridgeway YO26	16	C4
Ringstone Rd YO30	12	A2
Ripley Gro (Wig.) YO32	7	H1
Rishworth Gro YO30	12	A3
Rivelin Way YO30	12	A3
Riversdale (Haxby) YO32	8	C1
Riverside Cres (Hunt.) YO32	8	C5
Riverside Gdns (N.Pop.) YO26	10	C3
Riverside Wk YO1	4	D3
Riverside Wk (N.Pop.) YO26	10	C3
Riverside Wk (Stren.) YO32	9	F4
River St 6 YO23	5	E6
Riversvale Dr (N.Pop.) YO26	10	C3
Robin Gro YO24	17	G4
Robinson Ct 4 YO1	5	G4
Robinson Dr YO24	16	C5
Roche Av YO31	13	F5
Rockingham Av YO31	19	F2
Rogers Ct YO24	24	A1
Roland Ct (Hunt.) YO32	13	F2
Rolston Av YO31	13	F3
Ropers Ct (Cop.) YO23	22	C1
Ropewalk, The YO31	5	H2
Roseberry Gro 9 YO30	12	A2
Rosebery St YO26	17	G1
Rosecomb Way (Haxby) YO32	8	A4
Rosecroft Way YO30	11	H5
Rosedale Av YO26	16	D3
Rosedale St YO10	18	C5
Rosemary Ct YO1	5	G4
Rosemary Pl YO1	5	G4
Rose St YO31	12	D6
Rose Tree Gro (N.Ears.) YO32	13	E1
Rosslyn St YO30	17	H1
Rougier St YO1	4	C3
Roundhill Link YO30	12	A3
Rowan Av (N.Ears.) YO32	13	E2
Rowan Pl (N.Ears.) YO32	13	E1
Rowans, The (Skel.) YO30	11	F1
Rowley Ct (Ears.) YO32	8	C4
Rowntree Av YO30	12	D5
Royal Chase (Drin.) YO24	24	D1
Royston Cl 2 (Stren.) YO32	9	H2
Ruby St 1 YO23	18	A6
Ruddings Cl (Haxby) YO32	7	H3
Runswick Av YO26	16	C3
Rushwood Cl 2 (Haxby) YO32	8	B2
Russell Dr YO30	11	H5
Russell St YO23	18	A5
Russet Dr YO31	19	G2
Rutland Cl (Cop.) YO23	22	A1
Ryburn Cl 13 YO30	12	A3
Rycroft Ct YO31	14	B5
Rydal Av YO31	19	F1
Ryde, The (Skel.) YO30	6	A6
Rye Cl (Wig.) YO32	7	H3
Ryecroft (Stren.) YO32	9	F5
Ryecroft Av YO24	24	A2
Ryehill Cl 4 (N.Ears.) YO32	13	E1
Ryemoor Rd (Haxby) YO32	7	H3
Rylatt Pl YO26	16	C4

S

Sadberge Ct YO10	19	H4
Saddlebrook Ct YO24	24	A1
Saddlers Cl 1 (Cop.) YO23	22	B1
Saddlers Cl (Hunt.) YO32	13	G3
Sails Dr YO10	19	G4
St. Aelred's Cl 5 YO31	19	E3
St. Aidans Cl YO10	25	H1
St. Andrew Ct YO1	5	F3
St. Andrewgate YO1	5	E3
St. Andrew's Ct 13 YO1	5	F3
St. Ann's Ct YO10	18	C5
St. Aubyn's Pl YO24	17	H5
St. Barnabas Cl 10 YO26	17	G2
St. Benedict Rd YO23	4	D6
St. Catherines Cl (Skel.) YO30	6	B6
St. Catherines Pl YO24	4	A6
St. Chads Wf YO23	25	G1
St. Clements Gro YO23	18	B5
St. Denys Rd YO1	5	F5
St. Edwards Ct YO24	24	D1
St. Georges Fld YO10	5	E6
St. Georges Pl YO24	17	G5
St. Giles Ct 6 YO31	4	D1
St. Giles Rd (Skel.) YO30	6	A6
St. Giles Way (Cop.) YO23	22	B2
St. Helen's Rd YO24	24	C1
St. Helens Sq 3 YO1	4	D3
St. Hilda's Ms YO10	19	F3
St. James Cl YO30	11	H2
St. James Ct 4 YO26	17	H2
St. James Ms YO23	17	H5
St. James Pl YO24	17	E6
St. Johns Cres 7 YO31	18	C1
St. John St YO31	5	E1
St. Lawrence Ct (Hes.) YO10	26	D1
St. Leonards Pl YO1	4	D2
St. Lukes Gro YO30	12	C6
St. Margarets Ter 12 YO1	5	G4
St. Marks Gro YO30	11	H3
St. Martins La YO1	4	C4
St. Marys YO30	4	C1
St. Marys Cl 3 (Stren.) YO32	9	G3
St. Marys Cl (Wig.) YO32	7	H2
St. Mary's Cl 3 YO24	4	B5
St. Marys Gro YO10	19	H3
St. Marys La YO30	4	C1
St. Mary's Ms 5 (Wig.) YO32	7	H2
St. Marys Sq 15 YO1	5	E4
St. Marys Ter YO30	4	C2
St. Maurices Rd YO31	5	F2
St. Nicholas Av (Fulford) YO19	26	A5
St. Nicholas Cl (Cop.) YO23	22	A1
St. Nicholas Cres (Cop.) YO23	22	A1
St. Nicholas Cft (A.Bry.) YO23	22	B1
St. Nicholas Pl 4 YO10	19	E4
St. Nicholas Rd (Cop.) YO23	22	A1
St. Nicholas Way (Wig.) YO32	7	H2
St. Olaves Rd YO30	18	A1
St. Oswalds Ct (Fulford) YO10	25	H3
St. Oswalds Rd YO10	25	H1
St. Pauls Ms YO24	17	H3
St. Pauls Sq YO24	17	G4
St. Paul's Ter YO24	17	H4
St. Peters Cl 5 (Knapton) YO26	16	B3
St. Peters Ct 5 YO30	18	A1
St. Peters Gro YO30	18	A1
St. Phillips Gro YO30	12	B5
St. Sampsons Sq YO1	5	E3
St. Saviourgate YO1	5	F3
St. Saviours Pl 3 YO1	5	F3
St. Stephen's Rd YO24	16	D6
St. Stephens Sq YO24	16	D6
St. Swithin's Wk YO26	17	F3
St. Thomas Pl 4 YO31	18	B1
St. Thomas's Cl YO10	19	H3
St. Wilfrids Cl 2 (Stren.) YO32	9	G6
St. Wilfrids St YO1	5	F1
St. Wilfrids Rd (Stren.) YO32	9	G6
St. Wulstans Cl YO31	13	F6
Salisbury Rd YO26	17	G2
Salisbury Ter YO26	17	G2
Salmond Rd YO24	16	C6
Sandacre Ct 1 YO26	17	E2
Sandcroft Cl YO24	24	B1
Sandcroft Rd YO24	24	B1
Sandholme (Haxby) YO32	8	B1
Sandmartin Ct YO24	24	B1
Sandown Ct YO24	17	E6
Sandringham Cl (Haxby) YO32	7	H4
Sandringham St YO10	18	C5
Sandstock Rd YO31	14	A6
Sandygate 7 (Haxby) YO32	7	H4
Sandyland (Haxby) YO32	7	H4
Sandy La YO19	15	F4
Sandy La (Haxby) YO32	7	H2
Sandyridge (N.Pop.) YO26	10	D4
Sargent Av (Bish.) YO23	24	D5
Saville Gro YO30	12	B5
Sawyers Cres (Cop.) YO23	22	B1
Sawyers Wk (Dun.) YO19	21	H1
Saxford Way (Wig.) YO32	7	G1
Saxon Pl YO31	13	F6
Scafell Cl YO30	11	H4
Scaife Gdns 10 YO31	12	D6
Scaife Ms 9 YO31	12	D6
Scaife St YO31	12	D6
Scarborough Ter YO30	18	A1
Scarcroft Hill YO24	18	A5
Scarcroft La YO23	4	C6
Scarcroft Rd YO23	4	A6
Scarcroft Rd YO24	4	A6

Scarcroft Vw YO23	18	A5
Scaudercroft (Dun.) YO19	21	H1
Scawton Av YO31	13	F3
School Cl (Skel.) YO30	6	B6
School La (Fulford) YO10	26	A2
School La (Hes.) YO10	19	G6
School La (A.Rich.) YO23	22	A4
School La (Bish.) YO23	25	E5
School La (Cop.) YO23	22	A2
School La (U.Pop.) YO26	10	C4
School St YO24	17	E4
Scott Moncrieff Rd (Tow.) YO32	9	H5
Scott St YO23	18	B5
Scriven Gro (Haxby) YO32	8	B2
Scrope Av YO31	18	D2
Seafire Cl YO30	12	B2
Seaton Cl 2 YO10	19	H3
Second Av YO31	19	E1
Sefton Av YO31	13	G5
Segrave Wk YO26	17	F3
Selby Rd (Fulford) YO19	26	A3
Seldon Rd YO26	17	F2
Seventh Av YO31	19	E2
Severn Grn (N.Pop.) YO26	11	F5
Severus Av YO24	17	E3
Severus St YO24	17	E4
Seymour Gro YO31	19	E1
Shallowdale Gro 5 YO10	19	H4
Shambles YO1	5	E3
Shaws Ter YO24	4	B6
Shelley Gro YO30	11	H5
Shelly Dr (Stren.) YO32	9	F4
Sherborne Gro 2 (Stren.) YO32	9	G4
Sheriff Hutton Rd (Stren.) YO32	9	G2
Sherringham Dr YO24	24	B1
Sherwood Gro (Acomb) YO24	16	C1
Sherwood Gro (Hunt.) YO31	13	G4
Shilton Garth Cl (Ears.) YO32	8	C4
Shipton Rd YO30	11	H4
Shipton St YO30	12	C6
Shirley Av YO26	16	D1
Shotel Cl 5 YO30	12	A5
Silverdale Ct YO24	24	B2
Silver St 8 YO1	5	E3
Sim Balk La (Bish.) YO23	24	C4
Simons Cl (Stren.) YO32	9	F4
Sirocco Ct 7 YO31	13	E5
Sitwell Gro YO26	16	D2
Siward St YO10	19	F4
Siwards Way (Hes.) YO10	19	F5
Sixth Av YO31	19	E2
Skeldergate YO1	4	D4
Skeldergate Br YO1	5	E6
Skelton Cl 2 YO30	17	H1
Skelton La (Wig.) YO32	6	D2
Skewsby Gro YO31	13	G4
Skiddaw YO24	24	A2
Slessor Rd YO24	16	C6
Slingsby Gro YO24	24	C1
Smales St YO1	4	D5
Smary La (Murton) YO19	20	D1
Smeaton Gro YO26	16	D2
Smith Cl YO10	26	B1
Smithie Cl (N.Ears.) YO32	8	A6
Snowdon Cl (A.Rich.) YO23	22	A4
Somerset Cl YO30	11	H2
Somerset Rd 6 YO31	13	E6
South Bk Av YO23	18	A6
Southdown Rd (Hunt.) YO32	8	C6
South Esplanade YO1	5	E5
Southfield Cres YO24	24	C1
Southfields Rd (Stren.) YO32	9	G3
Southlands (Haxby) YO32	7	H1
Southlands Rd YO23	18	A5
South La (Haxby) YO32	8	A2
Southolme Dr YO30	11	H5
South Par YO23	4	B5
South Vw Ter YO24	16	D4
Sowerby Rd YO26	17	E3
Spalding Av YO30	12	B6
Speculation St YO1	5	G4
Spencer St 3 YO23	4	D6
Spen La YO1	5	F3
Spey Bk YO24	24	A3
Spindle Cl YO24	24	A1
Spinney, The YO24	24	D2
Spring Bk Av (Dun.) YO19	21	G1
Springfield Cl YO31	14	A6
Springfield Ct 7 YO24	17	G4

Springfield Rd (U.Pop.) YO26	10	C3
Springfield Way YO31	14	A6
Spring La (Hes.) YO10	19	F6
Springwood (Haxby) YO32	8	A4
Spruce Cl 4 (N.Ears.) YO32	13	E3
Spurr Ct YO24	24	A1
Spurriergate 12 YO1	5	E4
Stabler Cl 1 (Wig.) YO32	7	F2
Stablers Wk (Ears.) YO32	8	C4
Staindale Cl YO30	11	H3
Staithes Cl 1 YO26	16	C3
Stakers Orchard (Cop.) YO23	22	B2
Stamford Br Rd (Dun.) YO19	20	D3
Stamford St E 5 YO26	17	G2
Stamford St W 2 YO26	17	G2
Stanley Av (Haxby) YO32	8	A5
Stanley St YO31	18	C1
Starkey Cres YO31	19	E2
Station Av YO24	4	C3
Station Av (N.Ears.) YO32	13	E2
Station Ri YO1	4	B3
Station Ri YO24	4	B3
Station Rd (Cop.) YO23	22	A2
Station Rd YO24	4	C3
Station Rd (U.Pop.) YO26	10	C5
Station Rd (Haxby) YO32	8	B2
Station Sq (Stren.) YO32	9	G4
Steeple Ct 8 (Wig.) YO32	7	G1
Stephenson Cl (Hunt.) YO32	13	F4
Stephenson Way 14 YO26	17	G2
Sterne Av YO31	19	F2
Stirling Gro YO10	26	B1
Stirling Pk YO30	12	B2
Stirling Rd YO30	12	A2
Stirrup Ct YO24	23	H1
Stockhill Cl (Dun.) YO19	21	G1
Stockholm Cl YO10	25	H1
Stockton La YO31	13	G6
Stockton La YO32	14	B4
Stonebow, The YO1	5	F3
Stonegate YO1	4	D3
Stonegate Wk YO1	4	D2
Stonelands Ct 5 YO30	12	B4
Stone Riggs (St.For.) YO32	15	F1
Stones Cl YO24	17	F5
Stonethwaite YO24	24	A2
Stoop Cl (Wig.) YO32	7	H3
Stow Ct (Hunt.) YO32	13	F2
Strakers Pas 7 YO1	5	F4
Stratford Way (Hunt.) YO32	13	F2
Stray Garth YO31	13	G6
Straylands Gro YO31	13	G5
Stray Rd YO31	19	G1
Strensall Pk (Stren.) YO32	9	E1
Strensall Rd (Ears.) YO32	8	D3
Strensall Rd (Hunt.) YO32	8	C6
Strensall Rd (Stren.) YO32	9	F6
Stripe La (Skel.) YO30	6	A6
Stuart Rd YO24	17	E5
Stubden Gro YO30	12	A3
Sturdee Gro YO31	13	E6
Summerfield Rd YO24	24	A2
Summer Gdns YO30	12	A5
Sunningdale Cl YO26	16	C2
Sunnydale (Haxby) YO32	8	A4
Surrey Way 2 YO30	12	A5
Surtees St YO30	12	C6
Sussex Cl YO10	19	H5
Sussex Rd YO10	19	H5
Sussex Way (Stren.) YO32	9	F4
Sutherland St YO23	18	A6
Sutor Cl (Cop.) YO23	22	B1
Sutton Rd (Wig.) YO32	7	F2
Sutton Way YO30	12	C5
Swale Av YO24	24	C1
Swann St YO23	4	C6
Swarthdale (Haxby) YO32	8	A1
Swinegate YO1	5	E3
Swinegate Ct 1 YO1	5	E3
Swinerton Av YO26	17	G1
Swinsty Ct 9 YO30	12	A4
Sycamore Av (N.Ears.) YO32	13	F2
Sycamore Cl (Skel.) YO30	11	F1
Sycamore Cl (N.Ears.) YO32	8	A4
Sycamore Ct 11 (N.Ears.) YO32	13	F1
Sycamore Pl YO30	4	B1
Sycamore Pl 2 (N.Ears.) YO32	13	F1

Sycamore Ter YO30	4	B2
Sycamore Vw (U.Pop.) YO26	10	C4
Sykes Cl 3 YO30	18	A1

T

Tadcaster Rd YO23	24	D1
Tadcaster Rd (Drin.) YO24	24	C2
Tamworth Rd YO30	12	B4
Tang Hall La YO10	19	F3
Tang Hall La YO31	19	E2
Tanner Row YO1	4	C4
Tanners Moat 1 YO1	4	C3
Tarbert Cres YO24	23	H2
Tatton Cl YO30	12	B4
Teal Dr YO24	24	A1
Teck St 2 YO23	18	B5
Tedder Rd YO24	16	C6
Telford Ter YO24	18	A5
Temple Av YO10	19	G3
Temple Garth (Cop.) YO23	22	C3
Temple La (Cop.) YO23	22	B3
Templemead YO31	13	F5
Temple Rd (Bish.) YO23	24	D5
Tennent Rd YO24	16	C5
Tennyson Av YO30	12	D6
Ten Thorn La YO26	16	B3
Terrington Ct (Stren.) YO32	9	G2
Terry Av YO23	5	E6
Terry St YO23	18	B6
Thackerays Yd YO1	5	G5
Thanet Rd YO24	17	E6
Thatchers Cft (Cop.) YO23	22	B1
Theresa Cl (Hunt.) YO32	13	G4
Thief La YO10	19	F4
Third Av YO31	19	E2
Thirkleby Way YO10	19	H3
Thirlmere Dr YO31	19	F1
Thomas St 1 YO10	18	D4
Thompson Pl 13 YO26	17	F2
Thoresby Rd YO24	16	C6
Thorncroft (Dun.) YO19	21	H1
Thornfield Av YO31	13	G5
Thornfield Dr YO31	13	F4
Thornhills (Haxby) YO32	8	C2
Thorn Nook YO31	13	F5
Thornton Moor Cl 6 YO30	12	A3
Thorntree Gro YO30	12	B3
Thornwood Covert YO24	18	D6
Thorpe St YO23	18	A5
Tilmire Cl YO10	26	B1
Tisbury Rd YO26	17	F3
Tithe Cl YO24	16	C6
Toby Ct (Stren.) YO32	9	G4
Toft Grn YO1	4	B4
Top La (Cop.) YO23	22	A1
Toremil Ct 9 (N.Ears.) YO32	13	E1
Torridon Pl YO24	23	H2
Tostig Av YO26	16	D2
Tower Pl YO1	5	E5
Tower St YO1	5	E5
Town End Gdns (Wig.) YO32	7	G1
Townend St YO31	18	B1
Towthorpe La (Tow.) YO32	9	E1
Towthorpe Rd (Haxby) YO32	8	C2
Towton Av YO23	17	G5
Trafalgar St YO23	18	A6
Tranby Av YO10	20	A3
Trenchard Rd YO26	16	C1
Trenfield Ct 6 YO24	17	G4
Trent Av (Hunt.) YO32	8	C5
Trentholme Dr YO24	17	H5
Trent Way YO24	24	B2
Trevor Gro YO24	17	G5
Trinity La YO1	4	C4
Trinity Meadows (St.For.) YO32	15	G1
Troon Cl YO30	16	C2
Troutbeck YO24	24	A2
Troutsdale Av YO30	11	H3
Tudor Rd YO24	16	D5
Tuke Av YO10	19	G3
Turks Head Ct 3 YO1	5	E2
Turnberry Dr YO26	16	C3
Turners Cft (Hes.) YO10	26	C1
Turnmire Rd YO24	24	C1
Turpin Ct YO1	5	F5
Twin Pike Way 2 (Wig.) YO32	7	G2

U

Tyburn Ct *YO24*	17	H5
Tyneham Way **1** (Stren.) *YO32*	9	G4

Ullswater *YO24*	24	A2
Undercroft (Dun.) *YO19*	21	H1
Union Ter *YO31*	18	B1
University Rd (Hes.) *YO10*	19	E5
Uppercroft (Haxby) *YO32*	7	H3
Upper Hanover St **1** *YO26*	17	G2
Upper Newborough St *YO30*	12	D6
Upper Price St *YO23*	18	A5
Upper St. Pauls Ter *YO24*	17	H3
Usher La (Haxby) *YO32*	8	A2
Usher Pk Rd (Haxby) *YO32*	8	B1

V

Vale, The (Skel.) *YO30*	6	A6
Vanbrugh Dr *YO10*	19	H4
Vanbrugh Way (Hes.) *YO10*	19	F5
Varvill's Ct **3** *YO1*	4	C4
Vavasour Ct (Cop.) *YO23*	22	B2
Vernon Ct (Bish.) *YO23*	25	E6
Vernon Rd *YO30*	11	H3
Vesper Dr *YO24*	16	C4
Vesper Wk (Hunt.) *YO32*	8	C5
Vicarage Gdns **1** *YO10*	19	H3
Vicars Cl (Cop.) *YO23*	22	B2
Victoria Bar *YO1*	4	C5
Victoria Ct *YO26*	17	G2
Victoria St **1** *YO23*	4	D6
Victoria Way (Hunt.) *YO32*	13	F4
Victor St *YO1*	4	D5
Viking Rd *YO26*	16	D2
Villa Ct (U.Pop.) *YO26*	11	E6
Village, The (Skel.) *YO30*	6	A6
Village, The (Haxby) *YO32*	7	H2
Village, The (St.For.) *YO32*	15	F1
Village, The (Stren.) *YO32*	9	G3
Village, The (Wig.) *YO32*	7	G2
Village Garth (Wig.) *YO32*	7	H1
Villa Gro *YO31*	18	D1
Vincent Way *YO24*	24	A1
Vine St *YO23*	18	B5
Vyner St *YO31*	12	D6

W

Waggoners Dr **3** (Cop.) *YO23*	22	B1
Waincroft (Stren.) *YO32*	9	F5
Wainers Cl **6** (Cop.) *YO23*	22	B1
Wains Gro *YO24*	24	B2
Wains Rd *YO24*	24	B1
Walker Dr *YO24*	23	H1
Walmate *YO1*	5	G4
Walmgate *YO10*	5	G4
Walmgate Bar *YO1*	5	G5
Walney Rd *YO31*	19	F2
Walnut Cl (Hes.) *YO10*	19	F6
Walnut Cl **2** (Haxby) *YO32*	8	A2
Walpole St *YO31*	13	E6
Waltham Cl (Stren.) *YO32*	9	H2
Walton Pl *YO26*	16	C4
Walworth St **3** *YO26*	17	G2
Wandhill (Haxby) *YO32*	7	H3
Wandle, The *YO26*	16	B5
Wansbeck *YO24*	23	H3
Ward Ct *YO23*	4	D6
Warwick St *YO31*	13	E6
Wasdale Cl **10** *YO30*	11	H4
Waterdale Pk **4** *YO31*	13	F4
Water End *YO26*	17	F2
Water End *YO30*	17	G1
Waterings **3** (Wig.) *YO32*	7	G2
Water La (Dun.) *YO19*	21	H1
Water La *YO30*	12	B5
Waterman Ct *YO24*	16	C6
Watson St *YO24*	17	H4
Watson Ter *YO24*	17	H4
Wattlers Cl **7** (Cop.) *YO23*	22	B1
Waveney Gro **12** *YO30*	12	C5
Waverley St *YO31*	5	F1
Waynefleet Gro **3** *YO10*	19	F4

Weavers Cl (Cop.) *YO23*	22	B1
Weavers Pk (Cop.) *YO23*	22	B1
Weddall Cl *YO24*	17	G6
Welborn Cl *YO10*	19	F3
Welland Ri *YO26*	17	E2
Wellesley St *YO30*	12	B3
Well Garth (Hes.) *YO10*	19	G6
Wellington Row *YO1*	4	C3
Wellington St *YO10*	5	H6
Welton Av *YO26*	17	E2
Welwyn Dr *YO10*	26	A1
Wenham Rd *YO24*	24	A1
Wenlock Ter *YO10*	18	C6
Wensleydale Dr *YO10*	20	A3
Wentworth Rd *YO24*	18	A5
Wentworth Way (Hes.) *YO10*	19	E5
Werkdyke, The **6** *YO1*	5	F2
West Bk *YO24*	17	F4
West End (Stren.) *YO32*	9	F4
West End Cl (Stren.) *YO32*	9	G3
Westerdale Ct **1** *YO30*	17	H1
Western Ter **4** (Haxby) *YO32*	7	H1
Western Ter (N.Ears.) *YO32*	13	E2
Westfield Cl (U.Pop.) *YO26*	10	B5
Westfield Cl (Wig.) *YO32*	7	H2
Westfield Dr *YO10*	25	H1
Westfield Gro (Wig.) *YO32*	7	G2
Westfield La (U.Pop.) *YO26*	10	A4
Westfield La (Wig.) *YO32*	7	G2
Westfield Pl *YO24*	16	B6
Westfield Pl (Wig.) *YO32*	7	H2
Westfield Rd (Wig.) *YO32*	7	H2
Westholme Dr *YO30*	11	H4
Westlands Gro *YO31*	13	G6
Westminster Rd *YO30*	17	H1
West Moor La (Hes.) *YO10*	26	C1
West Nooks (Haxby) *YO32*	8	C2
Westpit La (Stren.) *YO32*	9	F4
West Thorpe *YO24*	24	B1
Westview Cl *YO24*	11	E6
Westwood La (A.Bry.) *YO23*	22	D3
Westwood Ms **2** (Dun.) *YO19*	21	H1
Westwood Ter *YO23*	18	A6
Wetherby Rd *YO26*	16	B4
Wharfe Dr *YO24*	24	B1
Wharncliffe Dr **4** *YO30*	12	A3
Wharton Av *YO30*	12	C6
Wheatcroft **1** (Stren.) *YO32*	9	F5
Wheatfield La (Haxby) *YO32*	7	H3
Wheatlands Gro *YO26*	16	D2
Wheatley Dr (Haxby) *YO32*	7	H3
Wheeldale Dr *YO32*	14	C3
Wheelhouse, The (Skel.) *YO30*	6	A6
Wheelwright Cl (Cop.) *YO23*	22	B2
Whenby Gro *YO31*	13	G4
Whernside Av *YO31*	19	F2
Whin Cl *YO24*	24	D2
Whin Cl (Stren.) *YO32*	9	G5
Whin Garth *YO24*	24	D3
Whin Rd *YO24*	24	D3
Whip-Ma-Whop-Ma-Gate **8** *YO1*	5	F3
Whistler Cl (Cop.) *YO23*	22	C1
Whitby Av *YO31*	13	H6
Whitby Dr *YO31*	13	H6
Whitecross Gdns *YO31*	13	E6
White Cross Rd *YO31*	13	E6
White Horse Cl **2** (Hunt.) *YO32*	8	C6
White Ho Dale *YO24*	17	G6
White Ho Dr *YO24*	17	G6
White Ho Gdns *YO24*	17	G6
White Ho Ri *YO24*	17	G6
Whitelands (Ears.) *YO32*	8	C3
Whitelands Cotts (Haxby) *YO32*	8	B1
White Rose Av (N.Ears.) *YO32*	13	E2
White Rose Cl (N.Pop.) *YO26*	11	F4
White Rose Gro (N.Ears.) *YO32*	13	E2
White Rose Way (N.Pop.) *YO26*	11	E5
Whitestone Dr *YO31*	13	F3
Whitethorn Cl *YO31*	13	F3
Whitley Cl *YO30*	12	B4
Whitton Pl **4** *YO31*	19	H3
Wigginton Rd *YO31*	12	D6
Wigginton Rd (Wig.) *YO32*	12	C1
Wigginton Ter *YO31*	12	D6
Wilberforce Av *YO30*	12	C6
Wilkinson Way (Stren.) *YO32*	9	F4
Willans Gro **4** *YO26*	17	F3
William Plows Av *YO10*	18	D5
Willis St *YO10*	5	H6

Willoughby Way *YO24*	23	H1
Willow Bk (N.Ears.) *YO32*	13	F1
Willowbank (N.Ears.) *YO32*	13	F2
Willow Cft (U.Pop.) *YO26*	10	B5
Willow Glade (Hunt.) *YO32*	13	G2
Willow Gro *YO31*	13	G6
Willow Gro (Ears.) *YO32*	8	D4
Willows, The **1** *YO30*	12	C6
Willows, The (Stren.) *YO32*	9	G4
Wilsthorpe Gro *YO10*	26	B1
Wilstrop Fm Rd (Cop.) *YO23*	22	A2
Wilton Ms *YO24*	17	G4
Wilton Ri *YO24*	17	G4
Wimpole Cl *YO30*	12	B4
Winchester Av *YO26*	17	F3
Winchester Gro *YO26*	17	E3
Windermere *YO24*	24	B2
Windmill La *YO10*	19	G4
Windmill Ri *YO26*	17	F4
Windmill Way (Haxby) *YO32*	8	B2
Windsor Dr (Haxby) *YO32*	7	G1
Windsor Dr (Wig.) *YO32*	7	F1
Windsor Garth *YO24*	17	E6
Windsor St *YO23*	18	A6
Winscar Gro **2** *YO30*	11	H3
Winterscale Ct *YO10*	18	C5
Winterscale St *YO10*	18	C5
Witham Dr (Hunt.) *YO32*	8	D5
Woburn Cl (Stren.) *YO32*	9	H2
Wolfe Av *YO31*	19	E2
Wolsey Dr (Bish.) *YO23*	25	E6
Wolsley St *YO10*	5	H6
Wolviston Av *YO10*	19	G4
Wood Cl (Stren.) *YO32*	9	F4
Woodcock Cl **1** (Haxby) *YO32*	8	B2
Woodford Rd *YO24*	17	E6
Woodhouse Gro **1** *YO31*	19	F3
Woodland Chase *YO30*	12	C4
Woodland Pl (N.Ears.) *YO32*	13	F1
Woodlands Av (Wig.) *YO32*	7	H3
Woodlands Gro *YO31*	13	H5
Woodland Way (Hunt.) *YO32*	13	G1
Woodlea Av *YO26*	16	D3
Woodlea Bk *YO26*	16	D3
Woodlea Cres *YO26*	17	E3
Woodlea Gro *YO26*	16	D3
Woodleigh Cl (Stren.) *YO32*	9	F5
Woodside Av *YO31*	19	F1
Wood St *YO31*	18	D1
Wood Way (Hunt.) *YO32*	13	H1
Woolnough Av *YO10*	19	G4
Worcester Dr *YO31*	19	G2
Wordsworth Cres *YO24*	24	A2
Wrays Av **6** *YO31*	13	F4
Wrays Cotts **5** *YO31*	13	F4
Wycliffe Av *YO10*	19	G3
Wydale Rd *YO10*	20	A3

Y

Yarburgh Gro **12** *YO26*	17	F2
Yarburgh Way *YO10*	19	H4
Yearsley Cres *YO31*	13	E6
Yearsley Gro *YO31*	13	E6
Yew Tree Ms (Osb.) *YO10*	19	H3
York Bypass *YO19*	26	D4
York Bypass *YO19*	14	D4
York Bypass *YO23*	24	D4
York Castle *YO1*	5	E5
York Rd (Dun.) *YO19*	21	E3
York Rd (Acomb) *YO24*	16	D4
York Rd *YO26*	16	D4
York Rd (Haxby) *YO32*	8	A4
York Rd (Stren.) *YO32*	9	G3
York St (Dun.) *YO19*	21	F2